CELEBRATING THE WILD MUSHROOM

CELEBRATING THE WILD MUSHROOM

A Passionate Quest

Sara Ann Friedman

Illustrations by Diana Jacobs

DODD, MEAD & COMPANY

New York

Published by Dodd, Mead & Company, Inc.
79 Madison Avenue, New York, N.Y. 10016
Distributed in Canada by
McClelland and Stewart Limited, Toronto
Manufactured in the United States of America

Designed by Claire Counihan

First Edition

1 2 3 4 5 6 7 8 9 10

Library of Congress Cataloging-in-Publication Data

Friedman, Sara Ann.
Celebrating the wild mushroom.

Bibliography: p.
1. Mushrooms.   2. Mushrooms—Folklore.   3. Mushrooms—
United States—Identification.   4. Cookery (Mushrooms)
I. Title.
QK617.F75   1986   589.2′2   85–27405
ISBN 0–396–08755–8
ISBN 0–396–08845–7 (pbk.)

CONTENTS

Contents

CONTENTS

ACKNOWLEDGMENTS

ALMOST EIGHT YEARS elapsed from the start of this book to its publication. During that time I built up a formidable pile of debts of gratitude to many people, and I want to thank some of them now.

First, there are my many mushroom friends from all parts of the country who shared their time, knowledge, hospitality, and their sense of adventure that is so much a part of mushrooming. Their stories and their passion confirmed that I was not the only obsessed mushroom nut in the woods.

And then there are Eric, Diana, and Michael, my three kids. They still hate mushrooms, but they put up with a lot of dinners "ruined" by their mother's morning pickings, and they tolerated the interruption of family softball games when I left my position in right field to look at a mushroom growing near third base. Victor, their father and my ex-husband, who went from bemused observer to enthusiastic hunter, was extremely sensitive, supportive, and helpful with the manuscript.

Charlotte Sheedy and Linda Nelson, my agents, showed a tireless faith in this book and stuck with it through "the worst of times." Anita McClellan, former Houghton-Mifflin editor, through her appreciation of the book's vision, helped me maintain my own. And I am especially grateful to Jerry Gross and Noah Pfefferblit, my editors at Dodd, Mead, for the meticulous care and attention they've paid to all aspects of this book—even for the hundreds of those little yellow query tags that decorated the manuscript for several months and made it a better book. The copy editor, Janet Biehl, was equally zealous and did a valiant job with the ever-changing Latin names of mushrooms.

Friends, colleagues, and members of various writing groups offered practical help and literary criticism. Among the many were Tony Astrachan, Bob Brannon, Bob Creas, Don Davidson, Arline and Walter Deitch, Elaine Edelman, Felicia Hirsch, Ursula Hoffmann, Ron Hollander, Marian Howard, Charles (CAM) Mann, Jo Ann Miller, Sue Mellins, Judy Speyer and Fran Shinagel. Three special friends—Gary Lincoff, Zach Sklar, and Bill Williams—each in his own way gave this book more help than even the best of friendships could demand.

And finally I want to thank Diana Jacobs for her enthusiasm, her patience, and her talent. Her wonderful drawings not only illustrate the text but also capture the spirit of the quest.

INTRODUCTION

Once I was standing at the base of a giant redwood in northern California. Huge branches, larger than whole trees in my eastern woods of birches and maples, crisscrossed in intersecting webs. There was no sky above, only more redwoods and the secrets of a thousand years.

Fleeting shadows, footsteps, and whispers broke the mood. Were they the murmurs of hidden forest creatures? The shadows turned into substance, the whispers into loud human voices. "Anything yet?" called one. "Over here," another answered. There must have been fifteen or more of them circling the trees, their eyes fixed on the forest floor.

A shaft of sunlight filtered through the tops of the trees and disappeared among the highest branches. *Look up! Look up!* I wanted to shout, but to my bafflement they were all on their knees, filling their paper bags and baskets with large white mushrooms. I could not help but laugh to myself at the sight of these frenzied foragers—a group of local mushroom hunters out in the woods on a singleminded search—who could not see the forest for the fungi.

Today my laugh would be touched with irony, for in the years since then I have become one of them, a mushroom zealot. My search for these fleshy fungi has taken me to the steep slopes of the Rockies, where I never looked up to see a snowcapped peak. And I am glad to have once seen the redwoods, for I now know that when I return, it will be on my hands and knees, nose to the ground.

In 1973, like most Americans I knew only two mushrooms; the one that grew in between the lettuce and the scallions on supermarket shelves; the other, a nuclear cloud. I knew that mushrooms could be fried, sautéed, broiled, chopped, and sliced, but it never occurred to me that they could also be looked at or looked for. Summer camps and city playgrounds had formed the natural boundaries both of my own childhood and of those of my three children; I associated the word *wild* with animals, kids, Indians, and parties.

It wasn't love at first sight; in fact, I'm not even sure where my obsession began. For years I had ignored or absentmindedly kicked over the hundreds of wild mushrooms growing in eastern Long Island, where my family and I had a summer home. One weekend, a houseguest brought me as a joke a small, delicate mushroom book from Czechoslovakia, on which she had written the inscription, "To my friend Sara who has everything." Suddenly I saw them everywhere, on my lawn and on my neighbors' lawns, in front of the public library and the town post office, in the dozens of local nurseries and in the sandy pine woods. I picked mushrooms and tried to match them with the pictures in the book, but they all looked alike and none matched. I went back to ignoring mushrooms.

One fall day a friend and his wife came to dinner. He dumped armfuls of pungent, odd-shaped mushrooms onto the counter of my Manhattan kitchen. They were covered with dirt and insects that had crawled out from under the gills. "Black trumpet . . . bolete . . . blewit."

He described a dozen varieties, wiping them but not washing them clean. "A little dirt and a few insects," he said, "are better than losing the flavor." I was fascinated, and before long I came to know that he was right.

Then there was the family camping trip in the Maine woods, where I was lured from the trails by the bold colors and erotic shapes of mushrooms. To the impatience and dismay of my children, my hiking was more lateral and circular than forward. I began to look more closely at the mushrooms, feeling and smelling them, savoring the odor of sweet apricots, turning up my nose at rotten fish. Mesmerized by the endless variety and challenged by the captivating surprises of these ephemeral creatures, so firm and bright in the morning, mere globs of dank decay by evening, I acquired half a dozen field guides and began to learn what mushrooms grow under what trees, and I began to trust my knowledge enough to eat what I picked.

There are thousands of species of mushrooms in North America, many of which have very strange shapes and don't look anything like mushrooms at all. Resembling heads of cauliflower or coral, slabs of beefsteak, soccer balls, turkey tails, or icicles, they hang, protrude, and billow from tree trunks, leaf mold, dead logs, and stumps. (They also grow on bathroom floors, dead bodies, in woodpecker holes, and on other mushrooms.) Mushrooms have fanciful folk names like "witch's butter," "shaggy mane," and "bear's head." Some turn blue or red when they are bruised; others glow in the dark. (A World War I soldier wrote home to his wife, "I am writing to you from the trench by the light of five mushrooms.") Seemingly small and fragile species have been known to push through slabs of pavement weighing a hundred pounds. Giant puffballs, fifty inches around, grow in a matter of days, and giant fairy rings of *Lepiota*,

Agaricus, or *Marasmius* have been known to continue growing for centuries. Many mushrooms are wonderful to eat; others are toxic enough to cause serious, if temporary, discomfort. Most are simply unpalatable, tasteless, or too tough to eat. A few are deadly.

The mushroom has played a role in nature, folklore, history, and religion. It has been feared and worshipped, and emperors have died from eating the delicate, seemingly innocuous ones. Ancient sculptors have immortalized its erotic form in stone. And the mushroom's magic has reduced at least one little girl named Alice to all but drowning in her own tears. It is no surprise that the mysterious appearance of mushrooms was believed to be the work of fairies' feet, dragons' breath, or thunder and lightning. The truth is another story and, as it unfolds, an even more imaginative one.

Like apples and tomatoes, mushrooms are fruits. The fruiting body, which produces the reproductive spores of the fungus, is attached to a mass of interwoven threads called the mycelium, which grows underground in soil, in leaf mold, or attached to the roots of trees and other plants. The mycelium functions somewhat like a plant or tree, from which the fruiting body of the mushroom grows. But unlike trees and other plants, the fungal mycelium has no roots, branches, leaves, or flowers. But then, of course, the fungus has never behaved like a normal plant, although it was once considered one. Ever since the early days of science, when the kingdom of God was neatly divided by scientists into animals and vegetables, the fungus has stubbornly refused to be pigeonholed. Lacking mobility, it is clearly not an animal; yet the fungus also lacks the quintessential quality that would make it a plant: the ability to use light and energy from the sun to produce its own food. Without chlorophyll, it cannot photosynthesize and must depend on other organisms for nourishment. In recent years, scientists have granted the fungus its own separate kingdom, equal in status to the other four: the Metazoan (animal), Metaphytan (plant), Procaryotic (bacteria), and Protistan (viruses).

Fungi inhabit every nook and cranny of the living world. By releasing an enzyme, they break down and absorb organic material into their own tissue. As a parasite the fungal mycelium attacks living trees or tree wounds as well as tissue in flowers, stems, leaves, and roots. One-celled parasitic fungi cause corn smut, chestnut blight, Dutch Elm disease, and wheat rust. Some fungi are saprophytes (the Greek word for "rotten"), nourishing themselves on the tissue of dead and decaying wood, leaves, conifer needles, dung, bones, and feathers.

As I ventured into this new kingdom, my eyes grew accustomed to the dark and I began to see how intricate and complex the world of fungi is, and how intertwined with our own. Without them, we'd be up to our eyeballs in fallen trees. Decomposing bark, leaves, and twigs, fungi clear the fields and forests of nature's clutter and turn decaying matter into nutrient-rich humus. Efficient waste disposers and major manufacturers of organic fertilizer, their success has not yet even been approached by the greatest human efforts.

Scientists have also learned that fungi play a vital role in the growth of many living trees. Forming mycorrhizae, or mushroom-roots, the mycelium takes carbon dioxide and other nutrients from the green part of the plant while breaking down cellulose and lignum in the soil and returning phosphorus, zinc, and nitrogen to the tree. Now, in their efforts to reforest and properly manage the ecosystem, scientists are finally paying attention to this important ancient relationship.

Fungi ripen cheese and ferment wine, and tiny fungal

yeast cells turn dough into bread by breaking down glucose and excreting carbon dioxide. And where would medical science be today if the common green mold called *Penicillium notatum* in the laboratory of Alexander Fleming hadn't gorged itself on the virulent bacterial strain *Staphylococcus?*

The fungus begins life as a spore, producing threadlike strands called hyphae that continue to grow, elongate, branch, and fuse until they become the mycelium. The mycelium, or fungal "plant," spreads in all directions, competing for space and food, penetrating whatever surface or substrate is rich enough to sustain it. Then there comes a time when the fungus must get on with the other business of survival: reproduction. Somewhere along the way mating, or simple nuclear fusion, takes place between two strands of hyphae, which then develop a new mycelium. Some fungi reproduce asexually; others reproduce without producing fruits or spores. But in those fleshy fungi we call mushrooms, a tiny button, containing a microscopic version of the fully developed fruiting body, develops on the strands of hyphae. The fruiting body pushes its way through the surface, and *voilà*—a mushroom. Above ground (or underground in the case of the truffle), the mushroom works quickly. Spores form on the gills, pores, teeth, or other surface; they ripen and fall. Carried in air currents and in the alimentary canals and on the tops of noses of animals, trillions and trillions of spores circle the earth, coming to rest somewhere, most of them dying; those that survive germinate to produce new mycelia. Its job done, the mushroom fades and disintegrates—within a matter of a week, a day, or sometimes hours.

Despite my background in classics and poetry, in history and art, and my own private *Sturm und Drang*, it took the primitive fungus to finally teach me that life

The life cycle of a mushroom

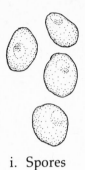

i. Spores

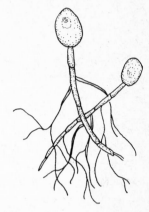

ii. The threadlike hyphae produced by the spores become the mycelium

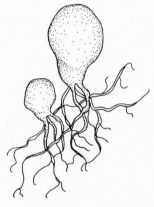

iii. Embryonic fruiting body

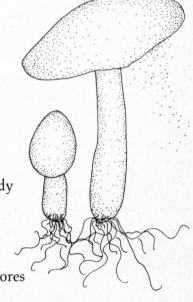

iv. Mature fruiting bodies (mushrooms) dispersing spores

and death are partners, inseparable parts of the same whole. Let others turn for comfort to their churches and couches; my acceptance of mortality has come from a mushroom, the once lowly subject of the plant kingdom that is now the ruler of its own domain.

Not alone in my devotion, I am part of a small but growing population of loyal subjects. There are thousands of us in North America and many more in Europe, where the gathering of mushrooms dates back to ancient times and has always been a family ritual. Among our ranks were such luminaries as Tolstoy, Lenin, and Freud. There are also celebrated (and obscure) cooks, painters, photographers, and fabric dyers for whom mushrooms are a subject of creative expression. There are seekers of altered states and seekers of altered tastes. Many learned the art of mushroom hunting from their European parents and grandparents; others discovered it while scouring the woods for other wild edibles. One woman I know came to it because her father had desperately wanted her to be a golfer, but she was so inept at fulfilling his dream that she kept hitting her balls into the rough, where she discovered mushrooms.

It is difficult to explain why these fungal fruits draw us into the woods, tempting us to forget time, ourselves, and our families. Looking for wild mushrooms allows us to satisfy without dire consequences those childhood urges that we are encouraged to bury. It allows us to get dirty. It gratifies our urge to steal. Crawling furtively through the woods, guarding our secret places, we fulfill our primal, competitive, and territorial drives. The search for mushrooms expands our world and leads us down new paths of knowledge, connections, and pleasure. Finding them allows us to retreat into private obsession. Anyone who has climbed the Himalayas or collected baseball cards, butterflies, or Mayan vases knows what it means to search for wild mushrooms.

Like most human passions, mushroom hunting involves excess and risk. In North America and Great Britain, the primeval fear of toadstools is proverbial, and sufficient to keep many off the mushroom trail. But an experienced mushroom hunter discovers that the danger of death lies only in a dozen species, while hundreds are safe, if not delicious, to eat. Careful identification makes the activity far safer than skiing. But there are other, more insidious dangers: the screech of tires and a possible three-car pileup, all for a twelve-pound chicken mushroom growing on a tree by the roadside. Sticking your hand in the duff under a pine tree is as likely to produce a slippery snake as a slippery jack, and roaming through the woods during open season on deer and quail is as likely to bring you face to face with a bullet as a bolete.

Adorned with dead stumps and rotting logs, my landscape is now perverse. Leaf mold and humus are my jasmine and honeysuckle, compost and cow dung my flowerbeds. The same two weeks of rain that fill my friends with despair fill me with joy and expectation.

There are no glasses left in my kitchen cupboard. They are all on the dining-room table keeping the draft from incipient spore prints. There is no longer any room to eat on the table.

There are days when a willow tree looks just like a bear's head fungus and the orange roof of a Howard Johnson's turns into a chanterelle. One night I fell asleep listening to a radio commercial; as my last conscious moment faded, I was sure I heard the announcer talking about a new species of mushroom called *Pholiota matica*. What he was touting, of course, was a *fully automatic* camera.

I have been hunting wild mushrooms since 1975. What began as mild curiosity has become an obsession. I have stalked the fleshy fungus from New York City parks and

Long Island lawns to the woods of Ohio, Texas, Oregon, Canada, and France. Along the way I have learned to follow the flow of a river, to name mosses and ferns, to observe the behavior of insects, and to use a microscope. I have learned to distinguish between deer dung and rabbit dung, not out of any scatological interest but because hidden among the leaves they look like small brown mushrooms. I have explored the myths of science and the science of myths. I have come to know a variety of extraordinary people, and I have come to know myself.

This book is about the joy of discovery and the frustration of fruitless search. It is about experience and knowledge. And it is, finally, a celebration of the wild mushroom itself.

CELEBRATING THE WILD MUSHROOM

Part I

THE HUNT

CHAPTER 1

The First Bite

People have been eating wild mushrooms for almost as long as they have been gathering roots and berries. And for probably just as long, they have been seeking to discern secret signs that would distinguish safe mushrooms from poisonous ones. Through myth and misconception, fear and prejudice, mystery and magic, that search for a simple truth has foundered and detoured. From down through the ages come aphorisms and admonitions of toadstools and tarnished spoons, of mushrooms that don't peel, and mushrooms that congeal milk or that turn onions blue and parsley yellow. Seeking comfort in rules and generalizations, ancient scholars of sophistication and intelligence attempted to turn folklore into scientific truth. For Horace, fungi that grew in meadows were best; he says it is well not to trust others. He tells us that "the nearer that a mushrome or toadstoole cometh to the color of a fig hanging upon the tree, the less presumption there is that it is venomous." And the ancient Greek physician Dioscorides tells us with great authority that poisonous fungi grow either among rusty nails or in rotten rags or near serpents' holes or on trees producing noxious fruits.

The simple truth is that there is no simple truth. For centuries, peasants in Russia and France have been picking mushrooms and discerning what they can and cannot eat by touch and look and smell, by knowing what grows where and when; they leave those they don't know alone and pass this information down to their children and grandchildren. Today, scientists use field guides, microscopes, and chemical tests. But in the end there is no way out but to study and learn the mushrooms themselves. Pliny the Elder knew this when he said, "When we are lacking in the botanical knowledge which most of us have neither time nor inclination to acquire, what course are we to take? Know one fungus from another as surely as one can distinguish between a carrot, a parsnip and a beetroot."

The final test of knowledge is, of course, in the eating, which may start with a chicken mushroom or with a hen-of-the-woods, two polypores (mushrooms with pores instead of gills underneath their caps) that are easy to identify; a puffball; a morel, if you can find one; a chanterelle, a shaggy mane, or a bolete—all are edible, tasty, and easy to recognize. If we have learned to tell a gilled mushroom from one with pores or teeth, to remember what grows on wood and what grows on the ground, to distinguish between a button *Amanita* and a puffball, and to take spore prints—and then, of course, to eat only what we know to be safe—no harm will come to us.

My first "real" mushroom was an *Agaricus campestris*, the common meadow mushroom or pink bottom, the closest wild relative to the cultivated variety that grows in the supermarket. I had previously participated in official hunting parties and forays, eaten at the tables of experts, and even picked and eaten my own edibles. But all had been guaranteed in person by attending mycologists or knowledgeable friends. On my own, I had hunted and gathered, dissected and discarded, described and drawn, examined and identified scores of mushrooms. But I had not yet eaten a single one of them and was eager to begin. And like many who come to something new in adulthood, I was frightened of making a mistake, knowing that it could be a fatal one.

I had already traveled the longest part of the road. No longer did I fear the wild mushroom as I still fear the treacherous undertow that pulls its hapless victims out to sea. Just as I had once been surprised to learn that gorillas are gentle vegetarians, so I was now surprised to discover the large variety of gentle wild mushrooms. I now laughed when strangers by the roadside cautioned me about eating toadstools. *Toadstool*, I explained patiently, is only a folk name for mushroom, springing from a primal terror deep within our cultural roots.

Still, doubts and questions lingered in my own mind. Experts sometimes disagree about what you can and cannot eat: the very same mushroom that is described as poisonous in one field guide is often described as edible in another. Every good species, it seemed, has an evil twin. Sometimes they grow continents apart: Laotians, Italians, and other foreign mushroom pickers have been known to land in hospitals in California, Oregon, or other new places after mistaking a poisonous species for one that is perfectly harmless in their own country. There are morels and false morels, chanterelles and false chanterelles. And then there is the small notice I saw in a local newspaper that read, CORRECTION: THE MUSHROOMS DESCRIBED IN LAST WEEK'S ISSUE AS EDIBLE WERE POISONOUS. And vice versa. Still, the neophyte mushroom hunter's fear eventually gives way to the need to know and the urge to eat.

One summer Sunday morning at about seven o'clock, the phone rang. It was my friend Richard, who had only just come home from a date. His voice was bright with excitement. "They're all over," he was saying. "Meadow mushrooms. Billions of them."

"You mean twenty?" I corrected, and forgave Richard his extravagance, knowing that he was a scientist accustomed to thinking exponentially. Richard was also a birdwatcher; he spent most of his summer afternoons on the beach with one eye glued to a telescope, scanning the horizon for migrating shearwaters. His other eye was usually on me, sitting on my blanket surrounded by field guides and the morning's collection of mushrooms carefully separated and protected by the sun in small wax paper bags.

One day, Richard arrived at the beach and casually dropped a large white object onto my blanket. "What's that?" he asked, pointing to it and cleaning his telescope lens.

I knew with barely a glance. "A puffball."

"Is it safe?"

"Of course."

"Then why don't we eat it?" He threw a Swiss army knife down onto the blanket and waited. I cut open the mushroom and showed Richard the inside, which was soft and yellowing with age. Tiny holes indicated the presence of insect larvae. "That's why," I explained. Richard returned to his search for shearwaters, a quest he viewed as having far more likelihood of fulfillment than did my desire to eat a wild mushroom. It didn't seem to matter to him that, as I had already explained a thousand times, I was neither cowardly nor stupid but simply careful.

"Billions of them," he was now insisting on the phone. I detected a defiant note in his voice as he told me of his plan to gather up and cook the mushrooms for breakfast along with some scrambled eggs and garden-fresh scallions. Did I want to join him?

"Wait a minute," I pleaded. "How do you know they're meadow mushrooms?"

"They're growing in my meadow. How else?"

How else indeed? He didn't know how easy it is for a novice like him to mistake a meadow mushroom for a deadly *Amanita virosa,* the destroying angel, nor did he know that *Amanitae* also grow in meadows if there are tree roots nearby to attach to.

Yes, he said, the mushroom was white, and it had a ring around the upper part of the stem—characteristics common to both the *Agaricus* and the *Amanita.* "But it's not an *Amanita,* if that's what you're thinking," he reassured me. The gills were pink, and there was no sac at the base of the stem. That made it a meadow mushroom for sure. Richard had learned his lessons well, and I complimented him on his observational skills. But surely he could wait until ten o'clock, when I would be awake and delighted to come over.

"I'm not waiting," he said. "But I'll be glad to save you some." Richard may have trusted me, but I didn't trust him. Nor was I inclined to diagnose or prescribe by telephone. I said I'd be right over.

We were two figures huddled in the hazy light, detectives looking for a murderer's footprints. Grass soaked with early morning dew wet our legs as we crouched over the clues. Carefully carving the earth from around a splendid young specimen, I removed the entire fruiting body and held it upside down in my palm. It was firm and fresh, and the gills had a definite pinkish cast, although it was pale and ephemeral. Peering through our hand lens, we found no remnant of a sac at the base.

We sat at the kitchen table, books and mushrooms spread out before us. "Where's your Peterson?" Richard asked, referring to the bible of birdwatching by Roger Tory Peterson. "There is none," I assured him, and went on to explain, in a slightly condescending voice, that there was no such thing as a definitive work on mushroom identification. The whole issue of positive identification,

I had already learned and was to relearn over and over again, had as much to do with interpretation as with information. Photographs, drawings, and descriptions varied as much from book to live specimen as they did from book to book.

Individual mushroom specimens vary as much as do the stripes of zebras grazing by the thousands on the Serengeti, which is why you need as many books as you can afford and you never rely on a single characteristic for identification. No indeed, I told Richard, the world of mushrooms offers little solace to seekers of the absolute.

I opened a field guide and turned to color photographs first of the meadow mushroom, *Agaricus campestris*, and then of the *Amanita virosa*. They were vaguely similar in size and shape. Both species have white caps, stems, and what are called "free" gills, which means the gills are not attached to the stem. Both have an annulus, or ring, under the cap, and both grow in grassy areas, although the *Amanita* needs tree roots while the *Agaricus* doesn't. There are differences, too: the gills of the *Agaricus* are pink, turning brown with age; those of the *Amanita* are white. The destroying angel has a sac at the base, while the meadow mushroom has none, and the *Amanitae* tend to be more slender and graceful. But even the differences can be worrisome: a white gill can look pink in a certain light, and the absent sac might simply have disintegrated underground; moreover, Richard's meadow, where the mushrooms were growing, was a large grassy area, but there were many trees nearby.

Reading aloud, I began to sense clearly that the mushrooms were *Agarici*. There was something about the texture of the cap, the dingy color beginning to form, and the shape and proportion of the stem and of the whole mushroom. It was a gymnast, not a ballerina.

Stop reading and look, I told myself. However much

it was part of my character to rely on books, I had learned that there was something equally, though indescribably, accurate in the *Gestalt* of the actual mushroom.

"You're probably right," I began.

"Great," Richard interrupted, getting out the frying pan. "You pick the rest, and I'll make some eggs."

"Wait a minute," I said. "We have to be *sure*."

"I thought you were."

"I am. What I mean is, we have to be sure we're right." Explaining to Richard that mushrooms are only grossly identified by the color of their spore prints, I cut a cap from a single specimen, placed it gill-side down on a piece of white paper, and placed a glass over the mushroom to prevent a draft. I told him that within a few hours, millions of tiny spores would oblige us by falling from the gills onto the paper, allowing us to examine their colors and helping us to identify the specimen. If the print were chocolate brown, we had an *Agaricus*; if it were white, probably an *Amanita*. If it were brown, I promised Richard, we would eat the mushrooms. If white, he would learn that paranoia is often the better part of good judgment.

To pass the time, I began flipping through some of my other books.

"What are you doing now?" asked Richard.

I acknowledged that though I was fairly certain that the mushroom was a meadow mushroom, I wanted to make absolutely sure of what it wasn't.

"My God," said Richard, "do you think that before I am able to identify a shearwater, I have to eliminate hummingbirds, penguins, and plovers? Not to mention pied-billed grebes and fifty species of gulls?"

"Of course not," I assured him. "But hummingbirds aren't poisonous, and you weren't planning to eat the shearwater, were you?

"Look," I said, "at all those white mushrooms." Facing us across the pages were dozens of fleshy white *Collybiae, Tricholomae,* the poisonous *Clitocybe dealbata, Lepiotae,* and representatives from almost every genus we had encountered and from many others that we had never seen in the flesh nor even heard of. Was there a poisonous species among them that closely resembled the meadow mushroom?

Calmly, I reminded myself of how far I had come in the last four years. I no longer needed a glossary for every second word; I knew which books to consult; I knew the difference between a pliant and a brittle stem. I knew immediately when a cap was striated or fibrillose, whether it was bell-shaped or umbonate.

I looked at my watch and rose nervously from the table. Removing the glass, I lifted the mushroom cap gently from the paper, and turned it over in my hand. In three hours, the gills had been transformed from a delicate, pale, hardly discernible pink to a deep, dark brown.

We both looked at the paper, with its sunburst configuration of feathery shapes in the richest, lushest, most delicious chocolate brown either of us had ever seen. I was convinced that our moment had finally come. "Congratulations," I said.

"Now?" asked Richard, no longer believing it possible.

"Of course," I answered, taking the frying pan from his hand. "Allow me." I poured in some butter and a tiny bit of oil, wiped the mushrooms with a paper towel, sliced them neatly, and placed them in the bubbling pan. "Wait a minute," I said, stopping.

"What are you doing?" asked Richard.

"Just checking, making sure these are all the same." I reminded him of the biologist who wound up in the hospital; a mixed bag of meadow mushrooms and destroying angels was discovered later in her refrigerator.

Richard stood at the stove, stirring gently. "Maybe you're right," he said as I joined him. "Mmmm," he murmured, tasting the first batch. "Maybe these aren't even mushrooms at all. Maybe they're a new strain of poison hemlock."

I looked at him and realized that I was again falling prey to my own fears. That I had heard those same stories a dozen times from a dozen different people. Sure, there were cases of mushroom poisoning, but there were also thousands of people who ate *Agarici* and honeys and bricktops and blewits and edible species of *Amanita* for years without ever making a mistake or being sick a day in their lives. If Socrates could take his medicine with a smile, so could I. Then, reaching into the drawer, I removed a silver spoon and put it in the corner of the pan, in accordance with an ancient test whereby if the spoon turns black, the mushrooms are determined to be poisonous. I knew it was only a superstition (and I wasn't about to wait for the results), but it couldn't do any harm.

I took a bite, savoring the superb taste as long as I could, swallowed, and smiled a smile of ecstasy.

CHAPTER 2

Morels, May Apples, and the Meaning of Life

MUSHROOM SEASON OFFI-CIALLY BEGINS in May, with the crack of a starter's gun in Boyne City, Michigan, where an annual hunt takes place. Undignified by mounts, unaccompanied by faithful dogs, armed only with bags and baskets, grown men and women creep along the forest floor in search of quarry that is neither fox nor rabbit nor quail: It is the morel. After the truffle, there are few foods more cherished by chefs and restaurateurs; few birds, insects, or flowers are more sought after or fought over by amateur naturalists. In spring, the salmon has its stream, the early bird its worm, and the mushroom hunter the morel.

As most mushroom hunters know, however, they don't actually *have* the morel. What they have is the convic-tion that somewhere out there, hidden among the poplars and old apple trees, sucking on the roots of a dying elm, they will find one or twenty or a hundred of this elusive, alluring fleshy fungus. But they are always also aware of the possibility that they might find none at all.

What is so special about the morel? What is it about this fungal fruit that emboldened Polish peasants during World War II to wander brazenly through German-occupied forests? That prompted German peasants of the nineteenth century, according to some stories, to set fire to their own forests because they knew that morels favored burnt-over areas? Why does it bring out the Captain Ahab in us?

Ask successful morel hunters where they find their bushelfuls, and they'll tell you, "Here and there." Ask where you can find them yourself, and their faces become large slabs of granite. Ask disappointed hunters why their catch declined from last year, and they quickly offer a cornucopia of excuses: It's still too early in the season. Perhaps too late. There hasn't been enough rain. Or perhaps too much.

The morel doesn't look like other mushrooms; it bears its spores in the pits and hollows of a cone-shaped cup instead of in gills or pores. The morel opens no doors of perception. It is safe to eat and has no dangerous look-alikes. Even the false morel, the *Gyromitra*, bears little resemblance to the morel and, although not recommended, is eaten safely in certain regions.

To be sure, the golden morel is lovely, its creamy honeycombed head hidden among last year's fallen leaves. But it is no lovelier than the chanterelle or the equally exquisite destroying angel. And although the nutty flavor of the morel lingers long after the rest of the meal is forgotten, it tastes no better than the parasol or the cep. So why the morel?

Because the season is short. It lasts only three weeks,

usually during May in the eastern United States (and at different times in other parts of the country), when the stinging nettle is four to six inches high, when the leaf of the may apple is unfurled, and when the bloodroot is blooming. It's the time when the oak leaf reaches the size of a mouse's ear, somewhere between the forsythia and the lilacs.

And because it is unpredictable. Although most mushrooms can be counted on to reappear in the same spot, the morel refuses to be pinned down. It is found on riverbanks and mountain slopes, in cow pastures and burnt-out forests, and under dead and dying elms, apple trees, and tulip trees, willow and ash. In sand and in mud. In New York and Canada and California. This year, everywhere; the next, nowhere.

The morel is a member of one of the two major subdivisions of fungi, the kin to the glamorous truffle, as well as to the thousands of tiny one-celled yeasts that infect our forests and ferment our food, and to the smuts, those purveyors of parasitic diseases. What distinguishes these Ascomycetes from gilled mushrooms, puffballs, polypores, corals, and most of the large fleshy fungi is their means of reproduction—the design of their spore-bearing structure and the style in which they give birth.

Most fleshy mushrooms are Basidiomycetes, members of the other major subdivision of fungi; they carry their spores exposed on the end of a microscopic, fingerlike projection called the basidium. Ascomycetes enclose their offspring safely inside a womblike structure called the ascus. When the spores are ready to be airborne, they are liberated by an explosive tear in the ascus wall that shoots them out like a jet of liquid. On a damp day, the ascus discharges its spores in a reasonably orderly fashion. On a quiet, dry day, however, a breeze, footsteps, or any other disturbance will cause large numbers of ripe asci to eject their contents at the same time, so that a thick cloud of spores is visible to the naked eye. If you place your ear next to a morel when it is giving birth, you will hear spores popping like a microscopic machine gun.

I have eaten morels, sharing the discoveries of others. I have heard that they grow abundantly scattered through the Northeastern woods. But I have never found them on the eastern end of Long Island, where I spend my summers, and it is unlikely that I ever will. An amateur geologist from the area once explained that we live on the wrong side of the moraine. The last ice age, which left the mainland and North Shore rich in loamy soil and giant, varied hardwood forests, ran out when it reached the doorstep of the south fork, leaving us with long stretches of white sandy beaches and only second-rate woods of scrub pine and oak. Those sandy beaches are small consolation when you're looking for morels. Richard, my birdwatching friend, promises that when he sights a golden-winged warbler around here, I will find a morel.

April 15. It is almost time to begin. People have been dropping *Verpae* into their conversations lately. *Verpae* are small, early, morellike mushrooms that poke their heads through the dead leaves, heralding the arrival of spring. By our Gregorian calendar, spring is already here. By nature's calendar, however, it is still on the heels of a long, cold winter and has got some catching up to do. Perhaps the *Verpae*, like the humans, have adapted to digital clocks and linear time and will be deluded into thinking it is indeed spring. I remember two Januaries ago, when it seemed that the forsythia and the dogwood had been fooled in such a manner.

The day is gray and windy, the temperature in the low forties. Brittle leaves crackle under my feet. The trees stand stiff and bare. I kneel, sinking into the cold, wet ground. A beetle scurries around my hand, miffed at the detour. I am relieved. There is life down there after all.

I crawl the length of a large dead trunk, examining it for future possibilities. One end is covered with dried-up turkey tails, those tough, ubiquitous polypores that survive meteorological holocausts and decorate logs and stumps from one end of the forest to the other. The middle section of the trunk is composed of large chunks of soft, red wood beginning to decompose. There is no other end. It has already turned back into the soft, wet soil, rich with humus and the odor of decay, ready to give life to other creatures as they once contributed to its own.

May 3. Still no word of morels, but the Washington, D.C., Mycological Society has scheduled its first walk of the season in the Northeast for this weekend. "Go," everybody says. It promises to be a beautiful weekend, but don't expect to find morels.

Along with twenty-five other loyal members of the club, I converge on the designated meeting place: the stonewalled entrance to a five-hundred-acre private preserve, recently opened for public use, some forty miles north of the capital.

The squadron leader is Kent McKnight, a highly respected professional mycologist who works for the U.S. Department of Agriculture. Perhaps a few impressionable morels will come out of hiding in the presence of such distinguished company.

McKnight announces his battle plan to the assembled troops. With the tip of the metal cane, he diagrams the terrain and divides us into two groups. Group one will head out along the high ridge across the road and circle around, concentrating on the area with sunny, south-western exposure. Group two is to follow its leader into the low, swampy area.

I stay close to Dr. McKnight. I have been told by friends that if there are morels to be found, he will find them. At the very least, the experience of walking with him will be rewarding. The morning is filled with conversation and discovery. A translucent blue-green newt lies motionless in the hollow of a stump. Dogtooth violets are beginning to bloom. We discuss the taxonomy of the genus *Limacella*, on which McKnight is working; the black-cherry gall virus; and the problem of defining color in mushrooms.

"With only the fruiting body to go on for field identification," he says, "color has always been one of the major taxonomic clues for a mycologist." Scientists began 150 years ago by separating families according to spore color; they often use the color of caps or gills to differentiate species. Mycologists themselves, he says, are the first to admit that this system of classification, based primarily on field characteristics, is a century behind the other biological sciences.

The mushroom, McKnight reminds us, had been placed in the kingdom of plants, like a duck cast into a family of swans; modern mycologists are chained to a system of identification designed for flowers and trees. After all, we are told over and over again, the mushroom is only a fruit. A berry or pear without a bush or a tree, its "plant" is the mycelium, buried and tangled under the ground and all but impossible to identify. This situation will probably remain until the taxonomy of fleshy fungi begins to attract more interest from government and industry. Only then can mycologists make real headway toward revamping this hopelessly outmoded, frustrating system.

That's why we mycologists throw up our hands with a mixture of pride and self-pity; we are forced to place so much emphasis on visible field characteristics such as shape, texture, gill attachment, and of course color. "It's too bad," McKnight goes on, "that mycologists aren't poets or painters or interior decorators. Then such colorful descriptions as 'robin's egg blue' or 'forest green' would be quite sufficient." But because a mycologist must be exact, McKnight is working to improve the existing color chart that is used by the National Bureau of Standards.

We talk some more about the ambiguous nature of scientific progress. The trouble, he says, is that scientific classification is merely an invention of man, a device for creating discrete units out of a continuum. In nature, after all, one color blends imperceptibly into the next. There are no neat lines like those the NBS devises. So it is with mushrooms: Most of them fall into a slim range of colors—earth tones of gray and brown—but in many different shades. McKnight is working now on how to improve the NBS's method by dividing and subdividing them into smaller and more precise groups.

We make our way along a stream. "This looks promising," McKnight indicates, pointing to a grove of tulip poplars on the edge of a mossy bank. But it doesn't seem so this time. I ask him how many species of morels there are. "That's difficult to answer," he says. "In France, fifty. Here, maybe five or six." "More morels in France?" I wonder. "No," he answers, "more mycologists working on them."

McKnight describes himself as a seat-of-the pants mycologist, but his back-home-in-Utah style belies an authority and a fierce demand for exactitude. At the end of the day, when nobody has found a single morel, McKnight apologizes and says it seems a shame that I came so far. I assure him that my trip was a success and that if morels had been there we would have found them. I know it is only a matter of time.

May 6. Heavy rains are followed by more cold weather.

Perhaps morel season will pass this year without morels. Perhaps there will be a summer without a spring.

May 9. Reports begin to drift in: Three morels have been found in New Jersey. Four on the North Shore of Long Island. A friend has just returned from the San Francisco area, where she says there were hundreds. But that doesn't count, for they are always abundant in northern California.

May 12. There is an old hemlock forest in northern Westchester called Mianus River Gorge. Due to the impact of farming and development, it is one of the last virgin tracts of hemlock in the East. Although no one I know has ever found morels under hemlocks, it is said that they are there.

The time is right, the day perfect. To ensure my success, I have forgotten all the necessary mushroom-hunting paraphernalia: basket, knife, wax paper, field guide. I am of the school that believes that only if you are unprepared will you find what you are looking for.

The trails are well-marked, with signs written along the edges identifying the flora: trailing blackberry, wild sarsaparilla, and false Solomon's seal. I glance leisurely at the signs, taking note of those that I am not familiar with. Then suddenly I realize I am reading the written signs and forgetting to pay attention to the plants themselves, like a museumgoer who rushes to the corner of each painting to identify the artist's signature.

But what do I know of may apples and bloodroot? Spring, for me, has always been for staring out of windows during final exams and going on crash diets before putting on new summer bathing suits. The woods have been for discussing Kierkegaard and telling ghost stories. Today, however, I regret the indoor pallor of my literary past, my erstwhile contempt for the mitosis and meiosis of high-school biology. Had there been but one science teacher who used the forest floor as a blackboard, perhaps I would now be as familiar with stamens and pistils as I am with objective correlatives and oxymorons. I want to rush home to my children, to hug them and warn them before it's too late. *Learn your families and your phyla*, I want to shout. *You won't appreciate it now, but you'll thank me for it later.*

At ten-forty-five, I am starved and ready for lunch. I want to empty my small bag so I can fill it with morels. I know they are here, more morels in this forest than there are drops of water in the oceans, than there are grains of sand on the beaches, more than all the stars in Hollywood. But I have not yet even seen a single mushroom.

The sun climbs higher in the sky. A blacksnake is coiled next to a large rock. Maybe the morels will come out to sun themselves, too.

Morning slips into afternoon, and still the edges of the trail bear no fruit. Like a child in a fairy tale, I am drawn deeper and deeper into the woods. Unlike in "Hansel and Gretel," there are no breadcrumbs to drop as clues to my whereabouts. But I am learning to read a new kind of map: the odd-shaped rocks and giant uprooted trees are imprinting themselves on my memory.

My feet hurt, and this isn't much fun anymore. Now is the time to find morels as a reward for patience. Ahead is a stone wall that winds around and around, leading perhaps to the gingerbread house of the witch. I know better than to follow it. Now is the time to find morels. I am turning in circles, obsessed with my singleminded search. I am lost.

May 18. I invite a spiritual friend to go morel hunting with me. Although she has never found morels, she has found truth and peace, and I am hoping that some of her success will spill over into my quest. I ask her to pray or make a request to her guru that I might find morels, but she refuses. My desire, she tells me, is too attached to "gross material objects." I explain that there are different kinds of spiritual truths and that finding morels would create for me the same kind of bliss that meditation has provided for her.

Instead of putting in a good word with her guru, my friend asks some neighbors in Connecticut for directions to an old apple orchard. We park the car and follow the left fork as directed, then another fork, and another. It eventually becomes clear that we are not going to find the orchard. This does not seem to bother her in the least. "If we are meant to find it, we will," she says.

Leaving my friend to sit on a rock, I wander off to find riverbanks and open wooded areas. When I return, exhausted, discouraged, and covered with black-fly bites, I find her exactly where I left her, feet dipped in the icy brook, her face flushed with bliss. "I see from your expression," she says smugly, "that you didn't find what you were looking for." "No," I answer wearily, "but I see from yours that you did." She smiles. "That's the thing about meditation," she says. "You're always guaranteed results. Maybe," she adds, "you're just looking in the wrong place." "Maybe," I answer, "if we had found that apple orchard, we'd be looking in the right place."

May 21. Reports continue to drift in from across the country. Everybody is finding bushels of morels. Housewives in Kansas and Iowa are tripping over them. They are selling them in the streets of Michigan. A man in my Edible Weeds class went on a birdwatching expedition to the Audubon preserve in Greenwich, Connecticut, and found two dozen "morals." He doesn't even know how to pronounce them!

May 28. I hear that a well-known New York food columnist was taken, blindfolded by morel hunters protective of their sites, to the perilous north end of Central

Park, where she was shown morels. I entice a neighbor to make the same journey with me. We keep our eyes open and find one red-throated warbler, one ritual shrunken lamb's head in perfect condition, and two suspicious-looking youths.

May 31. I remember what Kent McKnight said about morels favoring disturbed soil: they like not only burnt-out forests but also squirrel tunnels and bulldozed construction sites. There is plenty of construction going on here at the eastern end of Long Island. If the morel has been restricted by the ancient flow of ice, perhaps, like the herring gull and the cockroach, it will benefit from human progress and technology. If everyone else is finding bushels full, perhaps I will find two. But this also turns out to be wishful thinking.

Who are the people who find morels? Are they merely lucky? Are they people who substitute mushrooms for emotions? Or are they all, like fishermen, just telling stories? I think of three Japanese fishermen who stood next to me one July in the Middle Fork of Idaho's Salmon River, hauling in trout while I hauled in dead branches. They changed positions with me, one by one, so that I would be upstream and first in line. They each showed me how to flick my wrist, they exchanged their lures for mine, and finally one even gave me his fishing rod. Still they caught the trout, while I hooked my line to the edge of a rock.

Richard offers solace. "Don't despair," he counsels, and takes me to an open sandy meadow near his house, where he promises I'll see a sight that will make me forget morels. For the past ten dusks, Richard has watched a male woodcock appear from the thicket and perform an elaborate courtship dance. With great gusto, Richard imitates the strange, throaty "pe-ent-ing" sound of the bird and demonstrates the anxious suitor's strutting paces. I am impressed by his enthusiasm and unexpected tenderness, wishing only that a morel could be as constant as a woodcock. "When," I ask, "did you start loving birds?" Richard is amazed. "I never said anything about loving them. I'd just as soon eat a woodcock as look at it."

We sit waiting on a large rock as the orange sky turns gray. Once the blackbirds quiet down, he speaks in a whisper. It is very quiet. "Shhh," Richard cautions as I start to breathe. Gray turns to black, and still no sight or sound of a woodcock. Two night herons pass over- head. Richard looks at his watch and then at the sky. He is visibly upset. There is no point in waiting any longer. "Every day for the past ten," he mutters. "I just don't understand." "I do," I say.

June 2. It is no longer May, but spring is very late this year, and there is still a week or so left of hope. A man I know has just returned from the Berkshires with morels spilling out of his arms and the back seat of his car for the third year in a row. "I took all I could carry," he says, and provides me with precise directions to the Elysian cow pastures and apple orchards of western Mas- sachusetts. It is hard to believe such good fortune and generosity.

I arrange to visit an old schoolmate and her husband who live near Great Barrington. We find the entrance to an old abandoned orchard, where I leave my friend in the car nursing her new baby.

The thick underbrush makes it difficult to move or even see. I bend to part the heavy layers of poison ivy and tear at the catbriar thorns. An insistent chirping startles me from above. A male robin is huffing and puffing, hopping up and down on a low branch, his chest blown out as if he were about to burst. "I'm not interested in your nest," I tell him, "just show me where the morels are."

Tangled vines are choking the apple trees. Maples and hemlocks and hickories are squeezing them to death. The webworm is eating them alive. Under elm trees, where morels also grow, the *Ceratocystis ulmi*, a one-celled fungus and an Ascomycete like the morel, is responsible for the dread Dutch Elm disease. The fungus contaminates the larvae of the engraver beetle, which spends the winter under the bark and emerges in the spring covered with a sticky mass of spores. The adult beetles pass the fungus back into the trees by feeding on young branches and boring through the bark to establish brooding channels. Without the *Ceratocystis ulmi* to infect and break down the elm, without the beetle to provide housing for the fungus, the morel, which feeds on the roots of the dying tree, would have a far less secure existence.

How then is it possible to love morels without feeling somewhat ambivalent about their thriving at the expense of dying elms and apple trees? Harbinger of spring, the morel is also harbinger of death. It is time, I decide, to rescue my friend from her devouring baby.

At last I see it there in the shadows: a single, exquisite morel, almost six inches high, stands by itself, etched boldly against the edge of the orchard. I am afraid to move it. Perhaps it will fall apart at my touch. Perhaps it is only an illusion.

I step back and admire the spectacle for a moment. Stooping down, I run my fingers gently along the surface of the cap, in and out of the grooves and hollows, down the long rubbery stem. Carefully carving the earth from around the base, I remove the entire mushroom and place it reverently in the basket. I am giddy with hope; perhaps there are dozens, even hundreds, more. Trembling, I consider running back to the orchard and filling my arms with them. But scarcity teaches caution, even respect. Now that I have found them, it is enough to know that they are here and that I will return next year—but a week earlier!

Back in the clearing, a man with a pitchfork approaches me. "Whatcha got there?" he asks. Afraid that when he sees what I have he will reclaim his property with the sharp end of his implement, I reach tentatively into my basket and remove the morel. In those few moments, the head has been torn from the stem and is drooping like an injured sparrow. I cradle the wounded bird in my palm and hold it out to him. But all he says is, "Oh, a 'morelie.' We got plenty of them back there," and he points to the orchard from which I have just emerged. "You're welcome to them." It seems clear that this New England farmer knows nothing about mushrooms.

"I'm Polish," he continues, smiling. "Been hunting mushrooms four generations. Now if you want some-

thing really special, take the *prawdziwik*," he says, the Polish word for cep, or *Boletus edulis*, rolling off his tongue like butter. "Now that's the king of the mushrooms. They got morelies beat by a mile."

"Oh," I say politely but with little interest, fearing the possibility of my own disloyalty, "where do you find them?" He says, "They're all over." He gestures vaguely across the thousands of acres of Berkshire woods. "When do they come?" "July," he answers. "Maybe sooner. August, September too." I nod noncommittally and start to walk away.

"Come on back in July," he calls after me, licking his lips and rubbing the tips of his fingers together as if there were no words to describe the experience. "After that, you won't bother with *them* anymore." And we both look down at the poor, maimed morel disintegrating in my hand.

"Maybe I just will be back," I tell him, "to try this mushroom you rave so much about."

But I am still thinking about the morel, and realize that after July, it's only ten more months till May—a new season and a new chance to search for morels.

CHAPTER 3

Origins

IF MAY IS THE START of mushroom season, it is a false start indeed. June and much of July prove to be no more successful for finding other species than May was for morels. In the mornings I wake gloomily to still another cloudless blue sky. A sunbather's paradise, it is just possible that the rest of the summer will turn out to be a mushroom hunter's hell. I drag myself through the woods like a beggar poking among old trash. On some days I fill my baskets with bird's nests, asparagus ferns, and glass and pottery fragments from old garbage heaps.

I have discovered a new beech wood near the bay, and there is a thicket of scrubby pine nearby that bore rich and varied fruit last fall. Although it has not rained in several weeks and this July looks even stingier than usual, I keep looking. Winter-burned grass, not yet green, is already parched with summer thirst. The moss is an old army blanket, and the only touches of color in sight are found on discarded beer cans and McDonald's wrappers.

Then I see it. Poking through the leaves, not fifteen

feet away, a bright yellow flash catches the corner of my eye. Although I cannot tell much from this distance, it looks to be about the size of a fist. Perhaps a brilliant *Amanita muscaria*, which grows large and golden yellow in this area, or perhaps a species I have never seen. I approach slowly, my eyes riveted to the spot.

But my discovery turns out to be neither a mirage nor a mushroom. The only thing I guessed correctly is the size, for the object is in fact a reasonably new, bright yellow Wilson tennis ball. The color, I realize on closer inspection, is far more common to tennis balls than to any species of mushroom I know, and the Wilson is far more common in the woods this time of year.

A tennis ball! I turn it over in my hand and begin absently to pull off the leaves clinging to its underside. And there, under the sticky leaves, the fuzzy blanket has become a soft mushy substance, partly eaten away by a matted white mass of rootlike material. I wipe the substance off on my pants, regard the Wilson with disgust, and take aim to fire it as deep into the woods as possible.

But for some reason I don't release the ball. Poised, my fingers tighten around a new reality, one that I am only just beginning to grasp. For here in my hand, I am no longer holding a moldy, ratty tennis ball covered with mildew and decay. This white mass that sticks to my palm like excess suntan lotion rubbed in sand is in truth a complex conglomeration of hundreds and thousands of tiny strands or filaments—the mycelium of a fungus searching for food and survival, performing its incidental role in nature and perhaps producing a mushroom.

As agents of death and decay, lowly and mysterious in their origins, fungi have probably been objects of distrust and fascination for as long as we have known of their existence. Associated with snakes and toads and creeping crawling creatures of the mud, fungi have been judged by the company they keep, with elves and imps and witches and dragons, with thunder and lightning. So deeply interwoven are their roots in folklore and superstition that it has taken almost until the present day to disentangle them.

Classical scholars were intrigued and mystified by the origins of fungi. Astute in their botanical observations, they distinguished with ease between flowering plants and fungi; the latter, called *muketes* in Greek, have neither root nor stem nor branch, neither bud, leaf, flower, nor fruit, neither bar, pith fiber, nor vein, according to a pupil of Aristotle. To explain the frequent appearance of fungi after rainstorms, Plutarch argued that if soft clouds could produce deafening noises, and if flames could arise from the moist vapors in the air, then why, when lightning struck the ground, could not truffles or mushrooms spring into existence, too? Far away from Plutarch in time and distance are the writings in the Hindu Rig Veda, and the traditions in the highlands of Guatemala and in the Philippines of today, that intimate a close association between thunder and the appearance of fungi. Like most origin myths, those involving mushrooms have considerable basis in reality and can be explained by simple scientific facts—facts that often seem more mysterious and magical than the myths. Mushrooms actually develop largely underground. Stimulated by rain, they will break through the surface fully formed, appearing one day where a day earlier the ground was bare.

From Bohemia comes a different story of the mushroom's origins. As Jesus and Peter passed through the poor Czech villages, the story goes, the disciple disobeyed his master's order to take only bread and salt for nourishment. When Jesus confronted him as he was stuffing cakes into his mouth, Peter quickly spat out the mouthful and denied the whole thing. Ordered by Jesus to return and pick up the crumbs, Peter discovered that they had sprouted into mushrooms. Jesus then brought them as a gift to the poor: they were abundant but never filling. Properly admonished, Peter remained hungry.

Arising mysteriously from the bowels of the earth, fungi's association with dankness and decay stirred archetypal, often contemptuous rumblings among the early scientists. Nicander, a Greek physician, wrote of fungi as the "evil ferment of the earth." Pliny traced their origins to "mud and acrid juices of the moist earth." And the sixteenth-century herbalists of Germany and England, faithful to their classical ancestors, filled their own works with references to fungi as "imperfections of the earth," "earthie excrescensces," and "bastard plants."

Like every religion, Western science leans piously for support on its creation myths. And the lowly fungus played a prominent role in early thought about the origins of life: "Some plants have no seeds; these are the most imperfect and spring from decaying substances; . . . and

are unable to produce their like; they are a sort of inter-
mediate existence between plants and inanimate nature."
These words were spoken by a sixteenth-century herbal-
ist, Andrea Cesalpino, but his notion of spontaneous
generation dates back to Aristotle and formed the bed-
rock of biological thought about the origins of life until
the middle of the nineteenth century.

Although it was intended simply to explain the source
of all organisms whose birth could not be observed, Aristotle's writ of heterogenesis came gradually to justify
the isolation of certain lowly earthbound creatures whose
origins, it seemed, could only be explained by the process
of degeneration, corruption, and putrescence.

Still, every age has its innocent heretics who follow
their instincts relentlessly and without regard for consequences, upsetting preconceived notions and assumptions
that have ruled for centuries. In the case of fungi, they
were a handful of sixteenth-century scholars who refused to believe that seeds did not exist simply because
they weren't visible. As early as 1588, Giambattista della
Porta and several of his contemporaries observed fungal
spores with the aid of a simple lens. Delighted with,
though mistaken in, their discovery that spores are seeds,
they did not miss the far-reaching implications of their
simple observation. "Falsely therefore," said Porta, "has
Porophyrius said that fungi, since they do not arise from
seed, are children of the Gods."

But even such a modest refutation of established theory was ill-received, and almost a century later, in 1665,
one of the leading scientific figures of the day, Robert
Hooke, persisted in attributing the origins of fungi to
"any kind of putrifying Animal or Vegetable Substance
as Flesh," simply because he was unable to see "any such
thing as seed in any part of them." He was ahead of his
time in many ways; Hooke formulated a law on the

movement of elastic bodies, and his studies of fossil stratification anticipated some aspects of the theory of evolution by a hundred years. Although he invented the compound microscope, a major technical advance, and accurately observed the internal structure of larger fungi, when it came to the origins of fungi Hooke was caught in the web of ancient prejudice.

In 1688, Francesco Redi performed important experiments that proved that maggots grow from other maggots and not from rotten meat, thus establishing the theory of biogenesis, or life stemming from life. In 1729, another Italian, Antonio Micheli, similarly showed that fungal spores, not rancid melon, give rise to fungi. During the eighteenth century, mycelia were examined, more spores were observed, and basidia, asci, and sterile cells called cystidia were identified. In the 1760s, another series of complex experiments showed that molds arise from living spores and not from boiled vegetables. But it was not until 1864 that Louis Pasteur finally laid to rest the notion of spontaneous generation, or heterogenesis, by displaying incontrovertible proof that even those microscopic creatures called bacteria originate only from other living bacteria.

Off and on, the battles over fungi continued, waged by the soldiers, poets, barons, and county clergy who, along with physicians, were the biologists of the seventeenth and eighteenth centuries. Were fungi animals or vegetables? Neither, or perhaps both? Fanciful notion followed fanciful notion. Fungi were fragments of shooting stars or crystals condensed from the mucus of decaying leaves. Perhaps they were even transformed snails, according to J. Lyly, who said, "I am of this minde with Homer, that the Snayle crept out of his shell was turned eftsoones into a Toad, and thereby was forced to make a stoole to sit on, disdaining her own house." On the doorstep of the Age of Reason and the Enlightenment, the establishment dug in its heels.

As evidence of spores continued to mount, however, it became increasingly difficult to deny their existence. What they were and what they meant, however, were other matters entirely. Those who wanted to fit fungi into the plant kingdom continued to see spores as seeds and cystidia as flowers. Others, including the nineteenth-century fathers of modern mycology, Christian Hendrik Persoon and Elias Fries, still held the view that some fungi, at least, may originate by spontaneous generation. But although they were reluctant to relinquish old beliefs, they were also reasonable men, at least willing to believe what their eyes told them.

But if seeing is believing for some, for others it will always mean interpreting what you see to fit what you already believe. As the notion that fungi arise spontaneously from decaying and nonliving matter became impossible to defend, a far more imaginative way was found to prove their lowly origin. In the 1750s and 1760s, Baron Otto von Munchausen performed a series of experiments that resulted in some rather unusual conclusions.

Noting the "blackish dust" (spores) produced by old *Lycoperda* (puffballs), the baron placed some of the "dust" in tepid water and watched as the spores "swelled up and changed into oval, mobile, animal-like balls. These little animals (at any rate I will call them so because of their resemblance) move about in water; and when one observes them further the next day they form clumps of hard weft and from these arise moulds or fungi." The mycelium, he reported, which resembled white veins and roots, was actually a network of tubes in which these little animals roamed about. In other words, he declared unequivocally, "The fungus fruit body should not be viewed as a plant but as the dwelling place of innumerable tiny animals."

The tenacity with which scientific prejudice continued to demean the nature of fungi is notably evident in the support given to the baron's absurd ideas by one of his most ardent supporters, Carolus Linnaeus, an eighteenth-century Swedish naturalist and the father of biological nomenclature. Impressed by the baron's ideas, Linnaeus assigned the problem of fungi to one of his students as a thesis subject and repeated the baron's experiments himself. He saw and described thousands of little worms swimming in the same tepid water that two days before had been filled with the powdery spores of a common smut fungus.

Not only did Linnaeus agree with the baron's conclusions, he went so far as to propose a third natural kingdom for fungi. (Ironically, this third kingdom anticipated the present balkanization of the animal and plant kingdoms into five groups, although it had nothing to do with the absence of chlorophyll or the inability to photosynthesize, which are the current criteria.) In a subsequent edition of his important work of 1735, *Systema Naturae*, Linnaeus added a new, aptly named genus, called, *Chaos* (which included *Chaos fungorum* and *Chaos ustilage*) for the "mobile organisms" he had seen arising from the spores of fungi—"those thieving and voracious beggars," as Linnaeus describes them, "which seize upon the odds and ends which plants leave behind them when Flora is leading them into their winter quarters."

I know that Monday-morning quarterbacking is a dubious sport. I suspect that scientists of the twenty-second century will smile at our attachment to such primitive notions as DNA and black holes. And I accept that sharp critical faculties can be dulled by cultural bias. But I still wonder how a man like Linnaeus, known for his clarity of thought, a consummate classifier, an inventor of order, and a generous benefactor who bestowed on nature previously unheard-of tidiness, didn't wait to see whether the "vegetables" that had turned into "animals" would turn back into "vegetables" again. Was Linnaeus so committed to the purity of his botanical kingdom that, rather than see it contaminated by a fungus, he created a whole separate division? Or was it simply the age-old, oft-repeated folly of assigning an important task to a graduate student?

The biological origins of fungi are no longer disputed, but folklore about their origins goes on. Encircling the globe and tunneling back through centuries, myths have affected the literature, religion, and science of nearly every culture on earth. The written accounts of mushrooms date back to the Hindu Rig Vedas and to Sumerian clay tablets. Joseph's Pharaoh dreamt of fungi. Ancient Romans offered sacrifices to propitiate Robigus, the god of rust, a malevolent crop-destroying fungus. And today, British biblical scholar John Allegro, in his book *The Sacred Mushroom and the Cross,* goes to great lengths to prove that Jesus was the personification of the deity of a fertility cult based on the use of the mushroom *Amanita muscaria.*

The word *mushroom* appears to derive from several different sources. In Old French, it is *mousseron,* growing out of *mousse* or *moss.* In Welsh and Old English it is *maesrhum* (*rhum:* a bulge or bump; *maes:* in the field). Over the centuries, the Anglo-Gallic merging of roots has produced varied offspring that include *muscheron, muscheroms,* and *mushrump.*

Like archeologists digging through rubbish heaps in the field, anthropologists, ethnobotanists, and etymologists browse through thickets of linguistic underbrush hoping to find meaning in the mushroom rituals of India, Siberia, Guatemala, and Mexico. But no scholar has dug with more zeal for the cultural roots of mushrooms than Gordon Wasson, a retired banker.

Wasson has spent most of the last thirty years studying the cultural and linguistic history of mushrooms. In a remarkable collaboration with his wife, Valentina, *Russia, Mushrooms and History* (Pantheon, 1957), Wasson presents one of the most extravagant dichotomies of our time, dividing the cultures of the world into two classes: mycophiles and mycophobes, those who love and those who fear mushrooms. The Russians, Poles, Czechs, Hungarians, and high Germans, the Wassons tell us, share a love of fungi and the earth that is deeply rooted in their primeval past. At the same time, a giant fairy ring of mycophobic cultures encircles the North Sea, where the peoples of Norway, Denmark, the Netherlands, low Germany, and Great Britain share an equally deep morbid and primordial fear of fungi, for which they have provided a distasteful epithet: *toadstool.*

Here we have the beginnings of the mushroom's linguistic link to putrescence and danger and also, perhaps, to the scientific attitudes that condemned it to its lowly position for centuries. Determined to trace the word *toadstool* back to its original source, Wasson embarked on an etymological pilgrimage with all the fervor of a religious convert. He followed the trail through Irish, Anglo-Saxon, Old French, Italian, German, Russian, Slavic, and Greek, and back to the fountainhead of Western tongues, Indo-European.

In a dazzling display of etymological virtuosity, each turn of logic blending imperceptibly into the next, Wasson uncovered a kinship between fungi, toadstools, poison, frogstools, witchcraft, Satan in all his disguises, imps, filth, foulness, toadstools and stools of another sort, udders, sponges, and finally to the source of all life—the womb. Tracing, for example, the Latin word for poison, *toxicum*, he discovered that the Anglo-Saxons replaced the *x* with *sc*, forming their word for toad.

For Wasson, all linguistic roads eventually lead to the womb, although his roadmap is not always easy to follow. In a German linguistic variant, for example, *poggenstohl* means "frogstool." In regional Dutch parlance, *pogge* means not "frog" but "young pig," an animal known for its roundness, the characteristic shape of the womb. Wasson then moves to French; he tells us that *poche*, French for "pocket," is not so far from *pogge*, or for that matter from *pouch*. Altering his route, he discovers that the Slavic *gomba*, the German *Schwamm*, the Greek *sphongos*, and the Latin *fungus* itself are related and probably even derived from *wamb*, the Anglo-Saxon word for "womb," and from the Gothic *wamba*. In Irish, Wasson finds further connections between words like *bolg losgainn*, which means both "frog's pouch" and "fungus," and the Latin *bulga*, a humorous metaphor for "womb."

Sacs, pouches, bulges, and bellies suggest a thousand metaphors, most of which Wasson explores. One road that he leads us down takes us to sprites, imps, spooks, and Shakespeare's Puck. Along another route he connects the Italian *tosca*, or "toad," with the *Tasche*, "pocket" in High German. And he lures us up the garden path into a woods redolent with gaseous distension and collapse. Connecting one Puck with another, he tells us that the common name for "puffball" in Old Irish was *puckfist*, which means "a silent expulsion of hindwind." And from there, it is only a hop, skip, and a jump to dung, smut, and toad's excrement, where the *pixie stool* or *toadstool* of England is no longer something to sit on, but a metaphor for something else entirely.

According to Wasson, we find the roots of mycophobia

deep in the dark forests of northern Europe. The same swellings and wombs that the Russians and Finns and the peoples of the Mediterranean turned into lofty metaphors for the Holy Spirit and divine afflatus, the North Sea cultures reduced to sprites and an imp's flatus.

I placed the tennis ball in my basket, a poor substitute for a mushroom, and began to make my way home from the northeastern woods of the United States. How strange, I thought, that this round, fuzzy tennis ball should so closely resemble a bulge or a swelling. What, I wondered, quickening my pace, could be the Slavic derivation of tennis? The sun was beating down on my head, and it was time to go home. The forests of such musings are far too dense and dangerous for me to go any deeper.

CHAPTER 4

Amanitae *Everywhere*

A MIDSUMMER SPARSITY OF MUSHROOMS does not necessarily mean that nature's cupboard is entirely bare. There are always enough small brown mushrooms to engage the serious mycologist and enough scattered species to entice the neophyte with a hint of things to come. From early May, the mottled gray-brown *Polyporus squamosus* clings tenaciously in overhanging ledges to tree trunks. The elephantine strength needed to dislodge them is worth the effort only when the mushroom is very young and tender. In the spring, *Polyporus squamosus* is what we almost always find when we are looking for morels.

Closer to the ground but still on wood, *Tricholomopsis platyphylla* provides a creamy contrast to the dark forest furniture. Despite its frequent large size, its slender stem and chiffonlike gills give this bulky mushroom a delicate appearance. It is a mushroom that has been passed wantonly from genus to genus and thus may well suffer from an understandable identity crisis. Mild-mannered and anxious to please, its bland taste denies it a strong personality.

The legendary fairy-ring mushroom, *Marasmius oreades,* encircles my apple tree. I am not entirely convinced that mycelia, rather than elves or dragons, are responsible for this. I gather bushels of these small, delicate-looking but sturdy mushrooms and, together with *T. platyphylla,* dip them in batter, mix them in stews and rice dishes, and stuff them in grape leaves, knowing that they neither add to nor detract from the dishes I cook. I am fully aware that because there are slim pickings indeed in June and July, eastern mushroom hunters cannot afford to be choosy.

I learn to follow the streams and ponds and the watered places like cemeteries, nurseries, and the lawns in the more elegant sections of town. There in the woodchips of an elegant garden I discover dozens of *Stropharia rugoso-annulata,* a large, fleshy, somewhat tasty edible with purple-black gills and a ring; it far more closely resembles the *Agaricus,* the meadow mushroom, than it does the smaller, more colorful members of its own genus, *Stropharia.* Rare in the eastern United States until recently, *Stropharia* spores have been arriving by the scores on imported woodchips from the Pacific Northwest.

I learn that dung generates heat and retains moisture as it decomposes. Scouting riding trails and stables, I wonder: If *Stropharia* spores and mycelia can come in bags of woodchips, why not the hallucinogenic varieties of *Psilocybe* and *Panaeolus* in the bags of manure? The dung proves rich in the small, brown, inedible *Conocybes,* but little else.

Then, of course, there is the *Russula.* One of the first mushrooms we learn to recognize, it is also one of the first we learn to forget. Colorful to the eye and boring to the palate, the *Russula* is a hardworking peasant that evokes no romance, no folklore, no fear. From June to October, it grows like crabgrass on lawns, in woods, and on roadsides.

It takes a beginner to appreciate the *Russula*, for only the unjaded eye beholds with pleasure its coat of many colors. It is only the neophyte who smiles in delight after he has proudly filled his basket with fifty unknown specimens in brilliant shades of purple, red, yellow, and green, and they all turn out to be *Russulae*. The tightly packed, creamy white (but sometimes ochre) gills and the stout white stem evoke in the greenhorn a sense of familiarity, for even the beginner learns to recognize the *Russula* by its firm appearance and intense hues. However, the moment it is picked, the colors start to fade and the fabric to crumble. It is said that if you throw a mushroom against a tree and it shatters, you can be sure it's a *Russula*.

There are few poisonous species of *Russula*, and it is one of the few mushrooms for which taste is really the truest test. The few poisonous species are bitter, and all you need to find them out is a sensitive tongue and a precautionary pack of lollipops. A sharp bite through cap and gills should tell you within fifteen seconds whether to feed the *Russula* to friend or foe.

Once you have admired, identified, and eaten the *Russula* for a season or two, enthusiasm begins to wane. The mushroom's brightness becomes irrelevant. The novelty of cooking a mushroom simply because it is wild wears thin, and except in the case of the Russians, who cannot afford to let this mushroom, so abundant in their land, go to waste, and therefore cook them all, no *Russula* seems worth drying or freezing to use in winter soups and stews.

There is one midsummer mushroom that cannot be

ignored: the *Amanita*. Its brilliant hues of white and orange glisten on dull days. Its bold presence dominates fields and forests from June through October. If the morel is rare, elusive, and treasured, the *Amanita* is ubiquitous, brazen, and feared. It beckons seductively and, as Odysseus was drawn to the dangerous cliffs of Scylla and Charybdis, as the charmed Orpheus was drawn to his lovely Eurydice, as Hansel and Gretel were drawn to the gingerbread house, we too are drawn in our innocence to the *Amanita*.

There are several hundred species of the *Amanita* worldwide, with over fifty in the Northeast. Like the noble Medici of Renaissance Florence, the *Amanita* clan contains members that are violent and blackhearted as well as relatives that spread light throughout the world. The most beautiful, the most delicious, and the deadliest mushrooms are all members of this large and powerful family.

Records of the *Amanitae* go back to ancient days. The lovely, orange *A. caesaria*, with its pale yellow gills, was a deserving favorite of the Roman rulers. A cap or two of the treacherous *A. phalloides*, known also as the death cap, was reportedly slipped to the Emperor Claudius, thus making his best supper also his last. And it was no doubt the emperor's hasty flight to heaven that prompted his nephew and successor, Nero, to proclaim this pale green, sometimes brown-capped, sometimes white-capped, mushroom "food for the gods." But no species figures more prominently in the myth and mystery of mushrooms than the famed and fabled *Amanita muscaria*.

One of the easiest fungi to recognize, with its cap ranging from pale yellow to scarlet and covered with white patches, the *A. muscaria* is irresistible to poets, painters, and adventurers. Nine times out of ten, pictures in children's books that illustrate the "toadstool" are of the *A.*

muscaria. It was a fairy ring of *muscaria* that danced to *The Nutcracker Suite* in the film *Fantasia,* and it was no doubt the *muscaria* upon which the caterpillar perched, informing Alice that "one side will make you grow taller and the other side will make you grow shorter."

Derived from the Latin *musca,* "fly," the *muscaria* is also known as the fly agaric and has been used since medieval times to stupefy flies—it is either sprinkled with sugar or broken up and placed in a bowl of milk. Its power to stupefy humans as well has been documented for over three hundred years by eyewitness accounts of visions of ecstasy and by colorful rites practiced by certain tribes in Siberia.

Learning to recognize an *Amanita* is among the first experiences of a mushroom hunter. It is distinguished by its white spores; by its free, usually white, gills; by the volva, or sac, at the base of the stalk; and by its stately, elegant stature. Not all *Amanitae* have volvae, however. Some have enlarged bulbous bottoms instead, and a few have rootlike appendages. Most *Amanitae* have a ring, or annulus, that hangs like a torn skirt from the stem just under the cap, and many have distinct warts or scales on the cap itself.

No sooner have we taken our first tentative steps into the mushroom world than we are severely admonished to avoid all specimens with these characteristics. Although it turns out that only a handful of *Amanitae* are deadly, the *verna, virosa, phalloides,* and *bisporigera* are all very deadly species indeed. And although certain members of the family are edible and delicious, they are far too easily confused with their poisonous relatives. Avoid all *Amanitae*!

Then come further caveats: sometimes the ring disappears from the stem; the volva can disintegrate or be difficult to dig up from the ground; in older mushrooms, cap colors are extremely variable; gills are usually, but not always, free. Perhaps it is wisest, we are told, to avoid all white or even pale mushrooms. Avoid all beautiful mushrooms. Avoid all mushrooms.

Then one day we are initiates. There is no longer the danger of mistaking a chicken mushroom for an *Amanita*. We are absolutely certain, before cutting into a puff-ball, that it will not contain nascent gills, as an *Amanita* button does. We know before we take it that the spore print of an *Agaricus* will be chocolate brown. We can distinguish between the wedding ring of a parasol and the torn skirt of an *Amanita*. We are eating shaggy manes, chanterelles, and boletes and would be more than happy to eat morels. The *Amanita* is now isolated in its splendor, and we have come to know this spectacular mushroom only in order to avoid it.

Slowly, however, a headlong fascination with the *Amanita* creeps up on me. I have not yet participated, nor do I intend in the foreseeable future to participate, in any culinary intimacy with a member of this family. But eating, I decide, isn't the only thing. There are also the pleasures of aesthetics, knowledge, and intellectual challenge. And despite the mushroom hunter's firm denial of it, there is also a certain competitive urge to be known for the number of species you can identify.

Keeping a respectful distance from the *Amanita*, I determine to learn more about it. I want to know, for example, how to tell a *rubescens* from a *brunnescens* and a *flavaconia* from a *frostiana*. Our neighborhood is at this time filled with warted white *Amanitae*; their caps are covered with a chalky substance that comes off in your hand. Instead of a ring, fragments of a veil hang off the edge of their caps. Some of them smell of chlorine, and their bases look more like turnips than mushrooms. I know that although they are white, these *Amanitae* are neither the death cap nor the destroying angel. What are they?

But the woods and roadsides are overflowing with boletes and *Lactarii* (the latter in the same family as the *Russula*), and I postpone my scientific inquiry, dismissing these imposing creatures with a wave of the hand and a casual, "It's only an *Amanita*."

Weeks pass. Near my house there is a church and a cemetery. From my car, I can see more than a dozen mushrooms scattered through the grass and around the base of a large oak. Their caps range in color from yellow to gray-brown to deep brown, and they range in size from small buttons to flaring umbrellas. Many are covered with patches. Knowing they are *Amanitae*, I would ordinarily drive on. But for weeks there has been nothing better to hunt. I screech to a halt and wonder what they are. Are they one species or several?

The ground is hardened by the tenacity of grass roots, and as usual I am caught without a knife, a digging tool, a basket, or proper equipment of any sort. Still, I want these mushrooms. I know how important it is to remove the entire fruiting body from the ground, especially with *Amanitae*, for I have learned that the species are distinguished far more by the shape and texture of their bottoms than by their color, size, or any other field feature.

Unlike most other mushrooms, *Amanitae* are covered in their fetal stage by a protective membrane called the universal veil. As the button breaks through the surface of the ground, the membrane is torn; it hangs on in varying degrees of fragmentation. In the species where the veil is made of sturdy stuff, it remains at the base of the stem as a distinct volva, or cup. Sometimes the veil breaks up into patches on the cap and disintegrates at the base, leaving little more than powdery evidence that there was ever anything there at all.

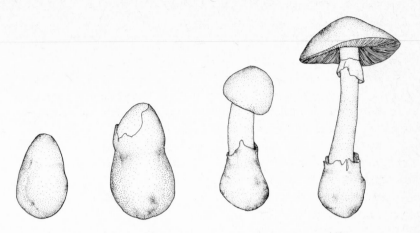

The developing stages of an *Amanita*

With the aid of a strong, sharp twig, I manage to re-
trieve a dozen more-or-less complete specimens. Today I
promise to forsake my usual haphazard and impatient
methods of identification and approach the problem from
a precise, scientific perspective. Knowing the spores will
be white, I still want to be absolutely certain; I take several routine spore prints. Using an index card for each
specimen, I record every observable feature without any
idea of its relevance: habitat, color, size, shape, texture,
cap, gills, stipe, and base. Is it glabrous or viscid? Tomentose or fibrillose?

The caps seem to be dry and are covered mostly with
scattered white patches. The gills are white and are mostly
free from the stipe. They all have a white, in some cases
pale yellow, ring. And although the bases vary, none
seems to have a saclike volva. So far so good. They are
all *Amanitae*.

I am immediately able to eliminate some of the more
familiar species: *verna* and *virosa* have pure, white,
wartless caps with archetypal volvas at the base. *Cae-*

saria, flavaconia, and *frostiana* are orange-capped. And *phalloides,* the death cap, which is rare in our area, fruits only in the fall and has a distinct sac at the base. None of my mushrooms smell of chlorine, have turniplike bases, or feel chalky to the touch, which eliminates another large subgenus, *Lepidilla.* And because they all have an annulus, I can also eliminate the other large group of ringless varieties, which used to be called *Amanitopsis.* As for *muscaria,* although the eastern variety comes in varying shades of yellow, I have never seen one without some remnant of a volval sheath around the stem. Besides, these just don't look like *muscariae.*

That leaves a dozen or so front-runners: *citrina, gemmata, rubescens, brunnescens, flavorubescens,* and *pantherina,* all of which have caps that range from white to brown and that are sometimes covered with patches. It also leaves forty to fifty other species common in North Carolina or Italy or Oregon, called by different names in different books, or not yet in any book at all, unnamed, perhaps even undiscovered. It makes me acutely aware of certain things.

1. My eyes are wedded to color. No matter how well I know that single species of mushrooms can vary enormously, no matter how hard I try, I cannot liberate myself from the relevance of shades and hues. The Eskimos have twenty words for *snow;* my designations of color variation slip and slide along the scale from *bleached-blond yellow* to *mustard-with-cloves* to *alarm-clock brown.* I am reminded of Kent McKnight and the National Bureau of Standards color chart and know that I am not the only one. Professional mycologists from the earliest days paid homage to spore color as the canon law of mushroom identification. And now, even as modern taxonomists are finding more subtle and complex evolutionary relationships in genetics and morphology, many are still reluctant to abandon color for more sophisticated tests involving chemical reagents and the scanning electron microscope.

2. The base of the Amanita *is supposed to be an important aid to identification.* Although no mushroom in my collection has an observable sac, in these twelve specimens I have seen every variation of basal shape from slightly knobby, to vaguely swollen, to what someone prone to flights of fancy might call bulbous.

A. virosa   A. pantherina   A. brunnescens   A. muscaria

Amanita bases

When does a swollen base become a bulbous one? Now this is the kind of question that makes me feel at home, but I know I am supposed to be defining mushroom bases, not interpreting them.

But if I think I have problems, a quick glance through the professional literature makes me wonder how anything ever gets identified. Landing on the monograph *Morphology and Subdivision of Amanita* by mycologist Case Bass, I see that he defines the different kinds of bases in the subgenus *Lepidilla,* those chalky white, chlorine-smelling *Amanitae,* with a kind of precision and poetry that I can only envy:

saccate
friable

layered
obliterate
pulverulent
floccose
lanose
crust forming
patch forming
wart forming
scale forming
circumscissile
ocreate
limbate
adnate
discrete

3. *There is more to mushrooms than color, shape, and texture.* Absorbed in minutiae, I find that previously unnoticed characteristics begin to appear. On the mushroom I am holding, I notice a faint yellow powder on the stem. I could swear it wasn't there before. How could I have missed it? Then I notice that all the stems seem to have bruised a reddish color. I have no idea whether this is due to the warmth of my fingers, whether all mushrooms do this on contact, or whether it is due to old age, exposure to the air, or total coincidence. It is impossible to tell what is important with mushrooms until you know them well. And once you do, it seems impossible that you ever didn't.

Based more on the small details than on the usual methods and rules, more on intuition than on knowledge, I have decided that these mushrooms are all a single species. The color of their caps varies; so do the shapes of their bases. But there is the ring and the yellow stuff, the reddish bruising on the stipe, and the look and feel of the entire fruiting body.

Selecting several caps, I scrape some spores onto a glass slide and add a drop of Meltzer's reagent, a part iodine-based, part chloral-hydrate compound that tests for the presence of starch and is used as an aid in identifying many kinds of mushrooms (as well as for other purposes unrelated to mushrooms). Spores that turn blue in response to the chemical reagent are said to have an amyloid reaction; those that do not are nonamyloid. Inexplicably, amyloid spores in *Amanitae* almost always come paired with smooth-edged caps, while the no-starch varieties have grooves, or striations, on their cap margins. I want to ask, Why? But *Why?* is a question for children and philosophers, and I must learn to phrase my questions in the language of science: *How* is the amyloid character of *Amanitae* related to a smooth edge? *What* is the correlation between grooves on the cap and the absence of starch? Perhaps the two characteristics are randomly linked on the same DNA strand. Perhaps there is no scientific correlation at all.

I watch as the spores turn blue, and then I return to the mushrooms to see whether the cap edges are striate or smooth. It is difficult to tell. The first one looks smooth. And the second. Then I begin to notice some gentle lines on the very edge of the third cap. They are more pronounced on the fourth. I return to the first. It is just possible—no, it isn't. If the spores turn blue, the margins cannot be grooved.

I am beginning to get the idea that identifying mushrooms is like playing a card game in which only the dealer knows the rules. Once you get beyond spore color and gill attachment, each genus has its own set of significant characteristics. In some, it is a question of whether the mushroom grows on wood or on the ground, on moss or under a specific tree like larch or red pine. In others, a genus will be defined by whether a cap is dry or viscid, whether the gills are serrated or smooth. In more and more genera these days, it is impossible to determine what chemical and microscopic characteristics they have in common with only a knife, a hand lens, and a reasonably good pair of eyes. Even within genera, rules change from year to year, as old characteristics are reevaluated and new ones discovered; whole groups of mushrooms are balkanized while others are unified. Names change and species cross borders from genus to genus. What was once a *Clitocybe* is now a *Lepista*, and *Pholiota* moves back and forth between the Strophariacae and Cortinariacae families.

Finally, my choices are narrowed to four: *rubescens*, *brunnescens*, *flavorubescens*, and *citrina*. They are all pale-yellow- to brown-capped, are amyloid, and possess a ring and a bulbous base. I eliminate *citrina* because it just doesn't seem right, and furthermore there is no odor of raw potatoes. Also, it is a fall mushroom. Like my specimens, *brunnescens* and *rubescens* both have reddish or brownish stains on the flesh of their stems, and they both have oval basal bulbs. The *brunnescens*, I learn, is distinguished by a cleft rather than by a simply bulbous base. Now I am back to the beginning. How am I supposed to know what a cleft looks like when I have never even seen one? A more unmistakable difference between the two species is that the *rubescens*, also known as the blusher, is edible, while the *brunnescens* is said by some to be poisonous. I suppose that if it finally boils down to a test between these two, that would be the surest way to tell the difference. But it will never come to that, for no field guide mentions yellow powder in connection with either of these two mushrooms.

Finally, I turn to *A. flavorubescens*. Many of the guides make no mention of it at all. A few distinguish it by yellow warts and patches on the cap, which my mushrooms do not seem to have. And one refers to a "volva, deep-yellow, quickly disintegrating in the soil around the base," but even there the author leaves it up to more expert minds than mine to translate the "disintegrating" volva into, perhaps, yellow powder (the same expert minds that already know the mushroom). Nor can I see much similarity between the picture in that book and any of my live specimens. If I am to exchange interpretation for fact and continue to believe in the myth of scientific precision, where is my answer? If eighteen of forty books in my house don't entirely agree about any mushrooms, save a dozen species that are obvious, if there is only one out of forty that clearly describes this seemingly common mushroom that I am holding in my hand, where is the comfort and security of science?

The mushroom does, anticlimactically, turn out to be *A. flavorubescens*. But not for another year do I know for sure, when a teacher in a class on mushroom identification that I am taking says with casual expertise, "There's one common *Amanita* around here which, because of the yellow powder around the base of the stem, you can't possibly mistake for any other."

It is two days later, and my specimens have decomposed, my index cards are filed. But I am crazed with power and longing to collect every *Amanita* in the area. Then come the rains. And they come and they come. Fairy rings of *Marasmius oreades* appear overnight on our doorstep. Dozens of *Gyroporus castaneus,* the small, tasty, chestnut-capped bolete, line the edge of our woods. There is edible *Lactarius* along the roadsides, and more boletes cover lawns and cemeteries. A friend brings me armfuls of the tiny *Cantharellus cinnabarinus.* But I ignore them all in my search for *Amanitae.* My refrigerator is full of them in wax paper bags, waiting to be examined. My oven is filled with them drying. Soon it is no longer fun, but I am unable to stop.

One day, riding my bike, I pass a young, brownish-capped *Amanita* on the roadside, a touch of gray warts scattered over the top. Is it a *brunnescens* or a *rubescens? Vaginata* or *inaurata?*

As I approach, a large, hairy black dog approaches from the other side. We regard each other until I turn away my eyes. He follows as I get closer to the mushroom. I look at him again and evaluate the situation. The dog has a lean and hungry look, but the empty orangeade container in its mouth renders it perfectly safe. I hope. I decide to continue my quest until the dog drops the container.

I move in, and so does the dog, pacing back and forth between me and my mushroom. I hesitate. This is total insanity; it's only a mushroom. But I must have that mushroom. I must know what it is. Possessed, I drop to my knees, digging furiously, and then finally climb back onto my bike, the *Amanita* resting in my basket. The dog drops the container and pursues me at a slow trot, gaining but never altering its pace. Suddenly, I know that I've seen that dog before, and I remember where. It was the devil's messenger in a horror movie I had seen a few years earlier called *The Omen.* Perhaps the *Amanita* has a power that extends beyond its beauty, beyond its toxic qualities. Quickly, I reach into my basket, hurl the mushroom as far as I can into the woods, and vow that if only I am permitted to escape, I will never again look at another *Amanita.*

CHAPTER 5

What's One Person's Poison . . .

Iɴ Jᴜʟʏ 1978, I ᴀᴛᴛᴇɴᴅᴇᴅ the Fifth Annual Conference on Mushroom Toxicology, held in Snowmass, Colorado. During the week, amid lectures on toxicology and taxonomy, I heard the tragic story of the death in 1944 of Julius Schaeffer, the well-known German mycologist. Financially destitute during World War II, Schaeffer was known to disappear into the local German woods for days at a time, collecting specimens for study and subsisting on nature's bounty. On one such occasion, Schaeffer was found dead by a colleague, a pile of mushrooms by his side.

Subsequent medical investigation and circumstantial evidence implicated a large, common, fleshy brown mushroom called *Paxillus involutus* that grows on wood and on the ground, in mixed hardwood and conifer forests. This species has a dull brown cap and brown, decurrent gills that run partially down the stem, giving a vaselike shape to the underside of the mushroom. But it is most distinguished by the inrolled margin of the cap, which accounts for its species name, *involutus*, Latin for "turned in."

This was neither the first nor the last account of mushroom poisoning that I was to hear. But as I thought about it, the incident seemed to epitomize everything I had learned so far about the dangers of mushroom hunting. Here was a mushroom, ignored in the eastern U.S., but eaten for years with relish and impunity in Europe and the Pacific Northwest, that has recently been discovered to contain toxins that under certain unknown conditions can cause sometimes-fatal liver, kidney, and/or heart damage in some people. In the Pacific Northwest, there have been no reports of poisoning by *Paxillus involutus*.

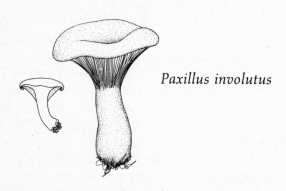

Paxillus involutus

It was a thirty-five-year-old story, but it was apparently important enough to be told twice during the same conference, first by a professional mycologist somewhere during a lecture on taxonomy, and later by an M.D. during a discussion of the diagnosis and treatment of mushroom poisoning. Its moral was obvious: "You can't be too careful," or "Even the experts make costly mistakes."

I was struck by the romantic image of the destitute mycologist ironically destroyed by the very substance upon which he seemed dependent for survival. Done in, so to speak, by the very thing he loved the most, by the fruits of his own labor, not unlike the Great Wallenda falling to his death from a high wire. Here was yet another example of the willfulness and unpredictability of mushrooms. A deadly toxin was suddenly imputed to an innocuous, not especially alluring species of fleshy fungus, eaten safely and enjoyed by some and ignored by others. The story had all the makings of a modern mushroom parable.

But I knew there had to be more to the story, some explanation that made sense, that didn't implicate the whole world of mushrooms in one poisonous species. A year later at another toxicology conference, held at the New York Botanical Garden, I got my answer. Biochemist Donald Symonds of Harvard related once again the tragic tale of Julius Schaeffer and *Paxillus involutus*. This time the story was followed by a diagrammed explanation. What happens, apparently, is that the mushroom produces antigens, which are enzymes or other substances that stimulate the production of antibodies in the blood. For years the body continues to fight back, producing those antibodies, until one day one final mushroom breaks the back of the body's defense system. Already brittle from the effect of the antigens, the red corpuscles rupture and the poison begins to take effect. The action of the toxin, Dr. Symonds pointed out, is cumulative. Death occurs only after many mushrooms and many years and not in every case. He also pointed out that Dr. Schaeffer was already suffering from a preexisting kidney disease, and so, although *Paxillus involutus* might have been a factor in his death, it cannot accurately be termed the cause.

It truly surprises most people to learn that of thousands of mushrooms, probably less than a dozen are deadly. There are, of course, scores that will cause sufficient grief to make you wish they were deadly, but in truth they are no worse than an overdose of prune juice. Understanding the nature of poisonous mushrooms will not make them edible, but separating reality from superstition is the better part of knowledge. Learning to distinguish between discomfort and the threat of death, between reality and imagined dangers, will turn irrational fear into intelligent caution and a risky adventure into a safe, but no less challenging, one.

The best-known and deadliest mushrooms belong to the genus *Amanita:* the brownish-, greenish-, or yellowish-capped *phalloides,* appropriately called the death cap, and the pure white *verna, virosa,* and *bisporigera,* which share the name "destroying angel." In addition to the *Amanitae,* there are several deadly members of the less-flashy, small, brown lignicolous (wood-growing) genus *Galerina,* and some small species of the otherwise-edible genus *Lepiota* as well. What these mushrooms have in common is nothing so ordinary as family relationship, size, shape, or color. They all contain amanitins, a particularly virulent group of toxins named for their most eminent carrier, the *Amanita,* and potent enough to put away a healthy, not particularly hungry, dinner guest.

It is not merely the presence of amatoxins (as amanitin toxins are known) that makes this group of mushrooms deadly, but also their concentration. Edible mushrooms like the chanterelle, the cep, and the blusher *(Amanita rubescens)* possess these toxins, but in such small amounts that an eater would die of gluttony sooner than poison. The amount of toxin in the death cap is twenty-five thousand times as great as that in the blusher, but even so, it takes at least a capful to put away an otherwise healthy adult.

This is not to suggest a *phalloides* feast, or even a nibble, but only to say that even the deadliest toxin has its threshold and to put to rest the popular notion that a touch is as treacherous as a bite. There is *no* mushroom toxic enough to contaminate other mushrooms close to it in a basket. No sniff, no touch, no backward glance will turn the cautious collector to stone. And there need be no more sleepless nights after forgetting to wash our hands between the collecting of a destroying angel and the cooking of a chanterelle. In the pot together, there is danger; in the basket, none—*just as long as you remember to throw out the poisonous mushrooms.*

Most cases of mushroom poisoning are cases of mistaken identity—a careless confusion of *verna* or *virosa* with large *Lepiotae* or with common meadow mushrooms, sometimes even with other, edible *Amanitae*. Unlike many other mushroom toxins, the amatoxins cannot be destroyed by cooking, and eating a misidentified *Galerina* or *Amanita* can be a serious, sometimes fatal, mistake. These toxins are heat stable, insoluble in water, and impervious to drying. No amount of boiling in oil or salt water will render them harmless.

Once it is ingested, the amatoxin is absorbed directly into the bloodstream, first attacking the liver. From there, the toxin advances to the kidney, where it does not exit through the urine, as many other toxins do, but is rather recycled through the bloodstream, creating further, often permanent devastation to the kidney and/or liver.

In the light of such determined virulence, it would be logical to assume mortality to be as certain as that caused by a bullet through the heart. Yet, to give the human body its due, the rate of survival without any medical treatment at all is said to be around fifty percent. Even the *Amanita phalloides* is not so sure a murder weapon as mystery writers and mycophobic historians would have us believe. Knowledgeable historians tell us that even the notorious death of the Emperor Claudius, who was executed so carefully at the behest of his beloved wife and his stepson Nero, by a reportedly delicious dinner of death-cap ragout, was secured by a pinch of powdered plant—the far less tasty, but certainly more deadly, bitter gourd *Colocynth.*

Unfortunately, the continued uncertainty and controversy within the medical profession about both the symptoms and the treatment of amatoxin poisoning contributes further to the confusion surrounding the lethality of these mushrooms. With less than four hundred cases reported annually and no more than six deaths, mushroom poisoning is hardly the number-one killer in the United States; there is little reason for busy physicians to familiarize themselves with the latest toxicological information or for biochemists to knock down doors to enter this field, despite some exciting research taking place on the behavior and structure of amatoxins. Although there are toxicology conferences, they are infrequent, and the same dangerous misinformation continues to be recycled through the same medical texts and journals. As the number of mushroom hunters increases, so will the number of mushroom poisonings, and one hopes that the involvement and education of physicians will also increase. In the meantime, it probably best serves serious amateurs to learn as much as they can about what might ail them, so that they can at least be prepared to pass that information on to the professionals.

The first clue to amatoxin poisoning may seem to be odd, but it makes a great deal of sense once the toxic action on the liver is understood. Although the onslaught begins almost as soon as the toxin enters the body, the symptoms usually do not appear until ten to twelve hours after eating the mushroom. Almost all the other, nonlethal toxins (for which no treatment is usually the best treatment) show their effects within one-half to three hours after ingestion and have completed their damage within six hours.

When they finally surface, amatoxin symptoms are severe. The very first description I read, in fact, was almost enough to end my interest in mushrooms just as soon as it had begun. Louis Krieger, in *The Mushroom Handbook*, delights his readers with the following:

> In from six to fifteen hours after the fungi have been eaten, the unsuspecting and unfortunate victim is suddenly seized with violent pains in the abdomen . . . being accompanied by excessive vomiting, thirst, and by either diarrhea or constipation. The pains may be so severe that the face becomes drawn, pinched, and of a livid color. The attacks coming on periodically, the patient soon loses strength, jaundice may set in and coma develops followed by death due to the extreme degeneration of the liver. Convulsions may or may not occur toward the end.

The second clue related to amatoxin poisoning is a dangerous truth that has been omitted from Krieger's graphic description: In between the first attack of agonizing pain, during which many victims wish for death itself, and the final stages of coma, jaundice, and complete degeneration, there is a day or two of apparent remission, which both patient and physician often mistakenly believe to be recovery. Many of the reported deaths occur three to six days after discharge from the hospital.

On the other hand, proper diagnosis and treatment, while they cannot guarantee complete recovery, have reduced the fatality rate of reported cases from 50 to 5 percent. Some say that if the correct treatment were used in every case, all fatalities could be eliminated.

Old myths die hard in medical school, as elsewhere, and one of the most tenacious myths concerns the effectiveness of atropine as a general curative for all types of mushroom poisoning—amatoxins included.

Atropine is an intriguing substance, rich in apocryphal history. An active compound found in such plants as jimsonweed, deadly nightshade, and henbane (all are of the belladonna group), it contains properties that are hallucinogenic. Medieval sorceresses were said to have rubbed the crushed plants, which were too bitter to eat, into the mucous membranes of their genital organs. One effect of this drug is the illusion of flying; this may account for the "airborne" feats of "witches" on their broomsticks. Whether the drug they used was atropine, scopolomaine, or some other alkaloid is open to question.

What isn't open to question, however, is that atropine contains curative properties as well and has been used with success for a long time as a homeopathic drug. When the toxin muscarine was isolated from *Amanita muscaria* in 1865, the drying and contracting effects of atropine were discovered to counteract the poison's symptoms: sweating, salivating, and tearing. Spurred on by their success, turn-of-the-century physicians enthusiastically endorsed the use of atropine to combat all kinds of mushroom poisoning. After all, their logic erroneously proceeded, atropine works for muscarine, muscarine is a mushroom poison, and once you've eaten one poisonous mushroom . . .

The century had barely turned, however, when it was discovered that *Amanita muscaria* contains only tiny amounts of muscarine and that it also contains ibotenic acid and muscimol, ingredients responsible for the delirious, trancelike state commonly associated with the mushroom. These compounds are not only resistant to but are also aggravated by atropine. By the 1930s, other toxins that had been isolated from other mushrooms also proved at best indifferent, at worst antagonistic, to atropine. Still, the drug continued to be administered as a general antidote. Even today, in the United States, it is the only mushroom medicine that most doctors know of, and its use continues to be recommended in outmoded medical texts. Outrageous as it may appear, mushroom poisoning is such a minor problem in this country that the medical profession neglects the subject and doesn't take the trouble to bring itself up to date.

What then is the appropriate treatment for mushroom poisoning? In most cases, surprisingly, no treatment is the best treatment. Since the majority of nonlethal toxins are gastrointestinal irritants and are usually self-limiting to about six hours, a good handhold and assurance that the patient will live are usually enough. Muscarine, which also occurs in many species of the small brown *Inocybe* genus and in the *Clitocybe dealbata* (called the sweater), is the only toxin for which atropine should be recommended.

As for the deadly amatoxins, no magic bullet has yet been devised to reverse their activity. But the poison behaves so much like viral hepatitis that informed doctors in this country are treating it as if it were, with continued supportive therapy, by the monitoring of blood chemistry for liver damage and hypoglycemia, and by maintaining the balance of fluids and electrolytes (salt and potassium) in the body.

In Europe, mushroom poisoning is a far higher medical priority than it is here. Over the years, serums and syrups have gone in and out of favor for treatment, along with milk, camphor, opium, and slippery elm bark. Among the more imaginative therapies in recent years has been the feeding of ground-up rabbit brains and stomachs to victims, predicated on the laboratory-observed evidence that rabbits have an inexplicable tolerance for *Amanita phalloides*. But this evidence turned out to be more wishful thinking than fact; rabbits' tolerance is only slightly greater than that of humans.

Another therapy has involved thioctic acid, a drug derived from lipoic acid, which occurs naturally in the body and plays a vital role in body metabolism. Since 1960, the drug has been widely used in Europe in the treatment of various liver diseases. In the United States, however, where proven successes with laboratory-tested animals are required before the FDA will release a new drug, the status of thioctic acid is still that of an Investigative New Drug (IND), and it is available only on special request. A small but intense controversy has arisen in this country over the issue of its general release. Proponents claim that fatalities can be completely eliminated; opponents claim that thioctic acid is the laetrile of the mushroom world.

The cure that has received the most press in Europe, however, is that devised by Jacques Bastain, the Linus Pauling of the mycological world, who travels the circuit and appears on television offering to eat *Amanita phalloides* in front of witnesses to demonstrate his "incontrovertible" proof that vitamin C cures not only the common cold but also amatoxin poisoning. Bastain also believes that amatoxins attack not only the liver but also the life-saving microflora that live in our intestines.

There are other mushrooms that are known to cause death, and surely still more that have never been tried or tested. But unlike the *Amanitae* and *Galerinae*, if some of these mushrooms are cooked properly, they may be eaten safely. Named for the brainlike convolutions of its cap, the *Gyromitra esculenta* is such a mushroom. (Also called the false morel, this mushroom looks very little like its treasured namesake. It has been suggested that the name was only part of a conspiracy to keep the number of morel hunters down.)

A popular mushroom in Europe and in the western United States, *G. esculenta* has been eaten for years with pleasure and impunity and has been sold in stores, fresh, canned, or dried. Yet some people do die from it. According to Gary Lincoff and D. H. Mitchell in *Toxic and Hallucinogenic Mushroom Poisoning,* "a very small percentage of the many who eat false morels suffer ill effects, but the mortality rate among those who do become ill has been reported to be between 14.5 percent and 34.5 percent." Looked at another way, this resembles my own favorite but less statistical life philosophy: all illness is either fatal or psychosomatic. Therefore, if you eat a false morel, you will either have no reaction or you will die.

For a long time, the action of *Gyromitra* poison, when it did attack, was a mystery on a par with the best detective story. Sometimes only one out of a group of ten who ate the mushroom would die. Sometimes only the cook, who ate none, would die. And there are reports of people who have eaten the *Gyromitra esculenta* for years suddenly becoming violently ill.

But then the mystery was solved. Some employees of the aerospace industry became ill with symptoms curiously like those of *Gyromitra* poisoning: an onset delayed from six to twelve hours, severe abdominal pressure followed by vomiting, and sometimes a permanent shutdown of the liver and kidney not unlike that caused by the amatoxins. It was finally discovered that the victims had been inhaling fumes of monomethylhydrazine (MMH), the same chemical that is used for fuel injection in space rockets. MMH is the toxin produced by the false morel.

It works like this. Through hydrolysis, the toxin gyromitrin is converted to MMH; its boiling point is 87°C. A sniffing cook can therefore get sick while an eater will suffer no ill effects. Boiling the mushroom sufficiently and discarding the water eliminates any toxic effect, but a mycophagist will suffer the consequences of this highly toxic mushroom sautéed, in soup in which the broth is kept, or otherwise improperly cooked. Olga and Mary Pesarick of Windsor, Vermont, have been eating *G. esculenta* ever since they were small children in Russia. After living in the United States for many years, they began reading books about mushrooms and discovered that it is deadly. Although they still eat the mushroom, they no longer give it to friends. When I asked them if they boiled false morels before eating them, they assured me that they did and were startled by my question. "Where did you learn that?" I asked. They shrugged. "Our mother always did it that way."

Further laboratory research with mice has also shown that the *Gyromitra* toxin contains carcinogenic properties, but still there is much that is unknown. It is not clear, for example, whether all species of *Gyromitra* contain similar amounts of toxin, and it is known that different individual mushrooms of the same species can contain different amounts of poison. Furthermore, because different species of the genus are often difficult to tell apart, it is not even clear whether Western and Eastern or American and European varieties are, in fact, the same or different species. In any event, even the invincible Charles McIlvaine, an illustrious amateur mycologist known for his iron stomach when it comes to eating mushrooms, advises against eating *Gyromitra* as a culinary treat in his well-known book, *One Thousand American Fungi*. "It is not probable," he says, "that in our great food giving country anyone will be narrowed to *G. esculenta* for a meal. Until such an emergency arrives, the species would be better left alone."

There is one more deadly mushroom that deserves attention: *Cortinarius orellanus*. Until the 1950s, *Corti-*

narius, largest genus of fleshy fungi, was considered to be edible, or at least was not known to be poisonous, since many species are not very tasty and are rarely eaten. Then a strange epidemic occurred in a certain region of Poland, where several people died from unknown causes over the course of a few years. Through dogged investigation, a physician discovered that the only thing the victims seemed to have in common was the eating of certain mushrooms. One of these mushrooms turned out to be *Cortinarius orellanus,* and because the toxin affects the liver in a slow buildup, it sometimes took up to two weeks for symptoms to appear, making it difficult to associate the illness with the mushrooms. It was discovered that *C. orellanus* grows in a single ravine in Poland, close to the area where all the victims lived and picked mushrooms. More toxic *Cortinarii* have been discovered since that time, and as many as a dozen species are now believed to be deadly; some of them grow in this country. Still, it is not a major worry for the North American mycophagist; we are talking about a handful of mushroom species in a genus that very few North Americans bother to eat anyway.

Although death is rarely a matter of opinion, one does usually need a body for proof. In the case of mushroom poisoning, there are far more deaths in fantasy than in reality, and many perfectly safe edibles have been condemned more by reputation than by proof of chemical toxicity. There is something unique about the passionate zeal with which stories of mushroom poisoning are accepted by the faithful and passed down from generation to generation—especially in this country, where the mycophobic tradition still runs strong. In our imaginations, there is no more savory ingredient for a sorcerer's elixir or a witch's brew than the virulent elixir squeezed from the flesh of a beautiful and deadly *Amanita.* There are hundreds of mushrooms that will make you sick to your stomach, sometimes violently, but the distress from very few, if any, lasts more than a day. Most of these are *Hebelomae, Inocybes, Entolomae,* and other undistinguished small brown mushrooms that we generally ignore. A few, however, resemble some of our favorite edibles just enough to lead the overly eager, unwary hunter right into an ambush.

The colorful jack o'lantern, for example, causes most of the minor poisonings in the East. Its orange color and vaselike shape often deceive the anxious chanterelle hunter. It is also confused with the honey mushroom: both are fall species that grow in clusters in wood. The jack o'lantern glows in the dark; it will also glow in your stomach, causing serious discomfort for several hours. Parasol hunters run the same risk when by mistake they pick the green-spored *Lepiota, Chlorophyllum molybdites.*

In lawns, parks, and other grassy areas, small white mushrooms grow in large concentric circles. One is the fairy-ring mushroom, *Marasmius oreades;* the other is *Clitocybe dealbata.* The former is edible, while the latter contains large amounts of muscarine and can cause profuse sweating and salivation, muscle spasms, reduced blood pressure, and a temporary slowing of the heart. One veteran mushroom picker thought he had picked and eaten the *Marasmius,* but shortly after dinner he began to sweat profusely and tremble. He went through his books until he discovered descriptions of the mushroom and his symptoms. The symptoms, the book assured him, would be over in five hours. He sat it out. The experience itself was not a pleasant one that he would want to repeat, but terror would surely have made it worse.

As thin-layer spectography and modern technology replace the silver spoon and other ancient divining devices, we learn more of the nature of toxic mushrooms; these techniques dispel myths and clear the reputations of some unjustly maligned fungi. In years past, for instance, the red-pored boletes were thought to be extremely dangerous. When I began to collect and eat mushrooms, conventional wisdom labeled them "toxic but not deadly." But today I know people who eat most of them, and I have myself done so with no ill effects. Has the mushroom changed? Have human beings adapted? No, we have learned.

A few red-pored boletes are known to be poisonous, even when cooked; others cause problems only when eaten raw or undercooked and must be parboiled or sautéed sufficiently to destroy the toxins.

Toxicity is also a matter of definition and degree. To some, the hallucinogens *Psilocybe, Panaeolus,* and the *Amanitae muscaria* and *pantherina* are toxic mushrooms to be assiduously avoided; to others, their hallucinogenic effects are more delicious than the taste of a chanterelle or morel. The body chemistry of some people enables them to eat certain mushrooms with impunity, while others will feel consistently under attack. Some of us can eat a mushroom once and be fine; the next time, a slightly larger portion might induce more than a full stomach. A few mushroom hunters react to the most common and safest edibles such as *Tricholomopsis platyphylla,* the giant puffball, and the chicken mushroom with diarrhea, vomiting, or swollen lips. But then, some people can't eat butter, and others break out in a rash from strawberries. The symptoms of allergies to such things as shellfish, ragweed, and cat hair are often more severe than the "poisonous" effects of certain mushrooms.

Pliny told us that to distinguish good from bad, we had to learn our mushrooms one by one, to know them like the backs of our hands, as we know a carrot from a beet from a potato. But knowing the names of the mushrooms is not enough. We must also know from experience or clinical tests that they are safe to eat and that they contain no toxins. But where did the ancient Romans turn for this information? Are our own modern books to be trusted?

The task of sorting out mushroom truth from lore is further complicated by simpleminded popular attitudes. In 1900, when the number of American field guides could be counted on one hand, amateur mycologist Charles McIlvaine called our attention to the superstitions surrounding mushrooms at a time when the word *mycophobia* had not yet been invented and when Gordon Wasson was probably not much taller than a toadstool. Riding horseback through the West Virginia mountains, McIlvaine was struck by "luxuriant growths of fungi so inviting in color, cleanliness and flesh that it occurred to [him] that they should be eaten." Which he did, before he had the chance to learn their names from books or with the help of experts. Locating some European publications, he traced the species, finding that many of them were listed as deadly. "As informed by these books, I properly ought to have died several times," said McIlvaine. The books were consistently inaccurate, and it soon became clear to him that they had only repeated each other in condemning the mushrooms, rather than testing their edibility for themselves. McIlvaine determined to do just that.

For twenty years up until, and some years after, the publication of *One Thousand American Fungi* in 1900, McIlvaine traveled throughout the country, collecting, recording, and eating mushrooms and recruiting "willing undertasters"; he built his list to seven hundred edible species. Among the seven hundred "edibles," however, McIlvaine included several dubious species: he described

Galerina marginata, for example, which is one of the undisputed deadly species, as a mushroom of "excellent quality" (in this case, it is possible that he had mistakenly applied this name to another species); *Clitocybe dealbata*, the muscarine-filled false fairy-ring mushroom, had "a charming flavor exceeded by very few other fungi." As for the jack o'lantern, the sworn enemy of the large intestine, McIlvaine "several times [had] eaten of it without other than pleasurable sensations," although he knew that "persons partaking of the same cooking had been sickened." As McIlvaine himself said, he "properly ought to have died several times." Why didn't he? This is a mystery left behind, paradoxically, by a dedicated dispeller of mystery.

McIlvaine's field guide was a major contribution to mycology. As he had hoped, it cleared away some of "the rubbish and superstition that have so long obscured the straight path to a knowledge of edible toadstools." Today, I eat many mushrooms that I was told were poisonous just ten years ago. Field guides are now appropriately cautious but are more restrained in their warnings, and experienced amateurs now trust themselves and one another to make their own tests.

But some of the rubbish and superstition remains, and one of the most dedicated and determined challengers of current poison lore is a full-time amateur named Greg Wright, a forty-year-old Californian, who says, "Things haven't changed that much since McIlvaine." Americans, he believes, are still dominated by old attitudes and fears that are not based on reality. Wright is engaged in a singlehanded and singleminded campaign to taste and test every species of "unknown" edibility. He doesn't eat mushrooms that in his view have been adequately proven to be toxic. But he insists on trying, at least once, almost everything else, including the foul-smelling, bitter, and unpalatable species, among them the green-spored *Lepiota* and the jack o'lantern, which have strong track records for making people seriously ill.

Wright doesn't just want to put more species in his mushroom stew; he is seeking knowledge. He wants to *know* the mushroom, and to him the flavor and the odor are as important to identify as the name. He can be seen at mushroom forays surrounded by the curious and the daring, a few of whom become his "willing undertasters." His major crusade is to clear the name of the *Amanita*. Most of us were taught to fear the whole genus, even though only a few species are dangerous. One of Wright's major triumphs was successfully challenging the reputation for lethality of *Amanita brunnescens*. Most of the field guides list it as poisonous, suspect, or unknown, but Wright has eaten it and gotten others to enjoy its asparaguslike flavor. Although Wright proved by this foray that, at least in some quantities, this mushroom is harmless, we still don't understand where its threshold of toxicity is or, indeed, if it has one.

His experiences, he admits, have made him ill seven times and have given him one good scare. But he shows no signs of slackening, and at last report he had tested over a thousand species. Some people admire Greg's seriousness of purpose; others think he's a little bit crazy. And there are those of us who see nothing at all odd in his behavior, since he is clearly a reincarnation of Charles McIlvaine.

All beginning mycophagists are a little like Greg Wright, eating the unknown. As McIlvaine observed, "The beginner at toadstool eating usually expects commendation for bravery, and fearfully watches for hours the coming of something dreadful." But with experience and knowledge, fear diminishes and self-confidence and the number of edibles increase. Our knowledge comes from many sources: the professional mycologists who identify the mushrooms, the biochemists who analyze the toxins, and the willing tasters who, cautious though determined, show—not tell—us what we can and can't eat.

CHAPTER 6

. . . Is Another's Meat

WAKE UP, IT'S AUGUST. It's nine o'clock and the month has nearly flown. The earth is piled to the sky with mushrooms.

Outside my door, the racket is worse than early-morning birds—screeching brakes, falling bikes, and churning driveway pebbles; shrieks and squeals and groans of ecstasy; things I can't make out. "Richard, your bird-watching friend, is here." My husband, Victor, pokes his head in the door. "He has something to show you."

"It's the biggest, fattest, orangest chanterelle I ever saw," Richard calls from the living room.

"Where'd you get it?" I ask.

"By the side of the road. On Town Lane, between my house and yours."

"It's not a chanterelle," I say.

"Then what is it? And how do you know without even looking?"

"How do you doctors diagnose on the phone? It's a *Hypomyces lactifluorum*," I mutter, pulling the pillow over my head. "Chanterelles don't—"

"Marie's here, too," Victor calls. "Richard met her at

the cemetery. And Jean called. She has some things she wants you to look at. I invited them both for breakfast."

I bury my head deep under the covers, pulling the pillow down with me. I hope she's not bringing a basketful of *Russulae*. Jean and Marie are both new mushroom friends. Marie is a professional cook of Italian descent. Her enthusiasm for mushrooms is a natural part of her heritage, and although her identification skills cannot be described as precise, neither does she come loyally bound to superstitions from the old country about what you can and cannot eat. She simply wants to eat *everything* that looks good enough. As for cooking, she seems to know intuitively, without ever having tasted a given mushroom before, how best to preserve its flavor and texture and whether it would go best in a sauce or a stew, dried or pickled, or simply sautéed in butter, sometimes with olive oil and a little garlic as well.

Jean comes to mushrooms via a more unusual route. Raised by the Jesuits, she was taught at an early age to avoid all eye contact. Looking down at the ground so much, she discovered mushrooms. Now a clinical psychologist, active feminist, and karate black belt, she still finds time for mushrooms and attacks them with the same energy she does her other activities. Her small house is filled with mushrooms and mushroom paraphernalia: glass-covered spore prints cover every table; index cards with drawings, descriptions, and measurements carpet the floor; strips of wax paper with specimens waiting to be examined and open books cover the chairs. The air is thick with spores and the aura of decay. In the corner stands an elegant binocular compound Bausch & Lomb microscope in the most beautiful shade of baby blue.

Like her house, Jean's basket is always filled to the brim: usually not, however, with fresh and luscious edibles, neatly wrapped and separated, but with small brown mushrooms, innocuous and inedible, shriveled beyond even a mycologist's recognition. Her boletes, when she finds them, are moldy and decayed; large holes and larvae indicate where insects have indulged in carnal and oral excesses. In fairness to Jean, however, fresh, young, unwormy boletes, numerous though they are, are difficult to find, at least on eastern Long Island. Among the fleshiest and tastiest of all mushrooms, their lifespan is considerably shortened not only by human hunters but also by hungry insects, and something about their spongy texture causes them to decay almost as soon as they are picked.

And *Russulae*. Jean's basket is never without *Russulae*, dozens of *Russulae*, in reds and greens and whites, crumbled and ratty, with clods of dirt and pine needles clinging to their bottoms. But Jean is more a collector than an eater, as insatiable in her curiosity as others are in their appetites, and like most beginners she is reluctant to leave *anything* in the ground, dirt and pine needles included. "I like *Russulas*," she said to me one day in a very assertive tone, "and you can't ask people to give up something until they're ready."

"I know because chanterelles don't grow that big." I am now answering Richard, face to face with his mushroom. "Besides, you found that in *my* spot." *Spot* is a mushroom hunter's euphemism for *territory*, and my reference is to a map Richard had drawn dividing up the area into proprietary territories. This beautiful, very large orange mushroom that actually does look more like a giant, malformed chanterelle than anything else grows on a particular roadside that falls onto my side of the map. I am now, you might say, accusing Richard of poaching.

"But that's right near my house," he tries to explain. "At least as close as it is to yours."

"It doesn't matter," I say. "That's a mere technicality."

Although herbivorous mushroom hunters do not all mark their territory in precisely the same manner, their sense of territorial propriety resembles that of the four-legged carnivore more closely than that of the bipedal property owner. In the case of the morel, and perhaps the cep as well, intrusion means a fight to the finish. With other mushrooms, the boundaries and codes of etiquette are somewhat more vague, depending to a large extent on the quality and quantity of the mushrooms to be found. As a birdwatcher, Richard has no sense of territorial propriety at all, and he does not understand my annoyance, even though, I remind him, it was his map.

"What's that?" asks Marie, about the large orange mushroom. "It's beautiful and so thick. I bet it would be perfect cut up in little chunks and sautéed with pepper and onions. Maybe a little zucchini," she adds, fingering the mushroom for texture, bringing it to her nose. "Can you eat it?"

"Of course," I answer, and explain that the mushroom is actually a *Lactarius* that has been parasitized by another fungus called a *Hypomyces*; hence the name, *Hypomyces lactifluorum*. This is not an uncommon occurrence among mushrooms, and many boletes, *Amanitae*, and *Russulae* are parasitized in this way. Some are edible, others are not. But there are no general rules about it; you just have to learn about each individual combination of fungi. In this instance, I am warming to my subject with the stunning orange color and the lack of gills.

"A parasite!" Marie says, handing the mushroom back to Richard as if it had stung her. "I'm not going to eat a parasite."

"You're not?" I ask. "What about your beloved honeys? And *frondosa*? And the chicken mushroom? They're killers all, sucking the lifeblood of the very trees that give them sustenance."

"But they're *funghi*," she says, lingering with love over the hard *gh* sound. *Funghi* means "mushrooms" in Italian and has none of the distasteful sound of the word *fungi* in English.

"So," I say, "is a *Hypomyces*."

In the kitchen, Richard is sorting through the piles of mushrooms. I am amazed at the quantity and variety of edibles that are spread out in front of him on the counter. Meadow mushrooms, young and fresh, their caps just beginning to open, gills unmistakably pink—no need for a spore print. Boletes of half a dozen kinds. Easy to distinguish from the gilled mushrooms, the spongy-bottomed boletes are difficult, if not impossible, to identify except for a certain number of clearly recognizable species. They are a nightmare for mycologists because they are so difficult to identify. For mycophagists, they are a pleasant dream, and it matters not at all what they are called. There is no group of mushrooms more savory, succulent, or safe. Of firm and fruity flesh, only a few species are poisonous, causing stomach upset in some people; these are a few boletes with red pores and a handful that stain blue when they are bruised.

A pound of chanterelles is spread out on the counter; their fluted edges are more than an inch across. "Oh," says Marie, rubbing her fingers along the blunt, gill-like edges, "little parasites." A beautiful cluster of oysters, they glisten like pearls and are plentiful enough for all of us to share. Richard is arranging the edibles in neat piles.

Exuberant from excess, Jean nearly bounces into the house and, finding us all in the kitchen, dumps her basket precariously near Richard's carefully arranged piles.

She sticks in her thumb and pulls out a tennis-ball-size puffball, the first of the season, pure white with large cracks on the surface, round and firm. The rest of us whistle appreciatively, and Marie suggests that perhaps we should cut into it just to make sure it isn't a giant *Amanita* egg.

"And," Jean grins, holding up for all to see a brilliant-yellow and orange chicken mushroom, neatly sliced from the base of a tree with not a speck of dirt or even a tough edge remaining, "there can't be any doubt about this." *True*, I am thinking; there is no doubt about the identity of this mushroom. The shelflike ledges give away this *Laetiporus sulphureus*, which is named partly for its polypored bottom and partly for its sulphurlike yellow color. One of the easiest edibles to identify, this parasite that attacks wounded trees can continue to grow for years on the same trunk, although it certainly loses its taste and texture if not picked in its first few days. A favorite of many experienced mycophagists for its strong and distinct flavor, it was described by a friend as tasting less like a mushroom than any other mushroom he knows. Tasting rather like chicken, the sulphur mushroom is sometimes substituted in chow mein and other Chinese dishes that call for chicken, just to trick the defiant, mushroom-hating child in every family. It can also be blended in a food processor and mixed with sour cream and a touch of sherry to be used as a dip or made into patties and served as sulphur burgers. Chicken mushrooms are usually found in large numbers, making them amenable to many ways of cooking, although simply sautéed in butter, sometimes with oil, garlic, and onion as well, and with salt and pepper, of course, its hearty taste and meaty texture can be superb.

The wonderful and terrible thing about cooking wild mushrooms is learning to understand their infinite variety of tastes, textures, and odors. Like zucchini, tomato, eggplant, and onion, each has its own distinctive personality and can be used to enhance the quality of bread, soup, quiche, and stuffing. The high art of mycophagy is often as overwhelming as the slightly lower science of mycology, as evidenced by local mushroom club activities: special cooking workshops and demonstrations, mycophagy corners in monthly newsletters, annual banquets, and wild food dinners. The fact is that there are probably more mushroom cookbooks than there are field guides, and more ways to cook a morel than there are morels. The discovery that individual human tastes can vary almost as much as mushroom tastes can be quite startling.

According to many, some of the most highly prized edibles, like boletes and morels, taste even better dried and reconstituted, which concentrates their flavor, than they do fresh. The aroma of dried boletes can be so fragrant that one New Jersey mycophile welcomes his dinner guests by sautéeing a small handful and simply letting the aroma waft through the house.

Chanterelles, on the other hand, although they are sold dry in specialty food stores, often lose their flavor by drying. They are adequate when sautéed but superb in sauces and stuffings. Some mushrooms, like the honeys, can be lightly sautéed and frozen, or pickled, to bring out their best. The blander edible mushrooms like *Russulae, Marasmius oreades,* and *Laccaria laccata* are used for their texture rather than for their taste in pancakes, stuffings, and rice-filled grape leaves. Of course, if you're Italian, none of this matters—it all goes on pasta; and if you happen to be Russian or Czech, it's into the pot of mushroom barley soup for all.

Like humans, mushrooms are close to 70 percent water. Tasty and filling, they add a great deal of pleasure, and

some bulk, to the best of meals. Whether they also provide nourishment is a matter of continuing debate. Some
say they are full of protein and vitamins; others say that
they are full of nothing. John Cage, composer and mycophile, set out to prove the former, subsisting for several days only on wild mushrooms; but he proved the
latter instead, to his great discomfort and disappointment. In any event, whatever nourishment mushrooms
may provide uncooked, it is most unwise to eat any but
a few species raw. Many contain toxins that are destroyed in cooking.

Most mushrooms should be eaten only when young.
Old mushrooms are not only tough, tasteless, and sometimes soggy, they are also likely to be the repositories of
thousands of tiny animals, and, like most aging food, to
release certain toxins in the process of decaying. Rarely,
however, do any of us follow these rules sufficiently.

The rest of Jean's basket, I have to admit, contains a
feast for both the eyes and the hungry stomach. Another
pound of chanterelles lies clustered in one corner of the
basket; a huge clump of inky caps leans against the side.
Clipped neatly across the stems, their fragile, umbrellalike caps and delicate white stems appear to be in pristine
condition. They cannot be more than minutes old, for
this mushroom is one of the most fragile of all. Within
a day, sometimes hours, the *Coprinus* deliquesces, or melts
away in parts, dissolving quickly into an inky black mass.
This is the way the mushroom releases its spores, rather
than discharging them by force or dropping them from
the gills, as other mushrooms do.

Scattered around the bottom of the basket are at least
twenty boletes, firm, fresh, and young, with not a single
bug, leaf, or twig in evidence. A varied assortment of
species, one or two are distinctly recognizable as the vivid

orange-capped *Tylopilus ballouii*, a large and fleshy edible that some people find delicious but that I think is on the bitter side; like the small chestnut-capped *Gyroporus castaneus* that grows like dandelions across our lawn, it is as reliable a breakfast companion from August through October as the daily-delivered *New York Times*. A wonderful little edible, robed in velvet and crowned by morning dew, it is not much taller than a week-old blade of grass. Prized by humans, it is even more highly prized by a variety of smaller creatures, especially after heavy rains, when a microscopic elf called *Hypomyces chrysospermes* dusts the mushroom with its parasitic white powder, giving it the appearance of a sugar-coated doughnut and making it inedible.

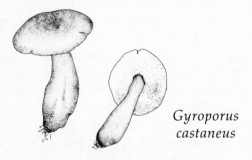

Gyroporus castaneus

"And not a single *Russula*," Jean says proudly, showing her empty basket.

We are all silent, carefully sorting, cleaning, and slicing the mushrooms, counting twenty-two edible species (in the East we make up in variety for what we lack in quantity), enough for a healthy taste for each of us. Victor, who had disappeared, returns, the bottom of his shirt overflowing with mushrooms. A self-professed mushroom cynic, as many husbands or wives of obsessive-compulsive hunters are, Victor attempts to disguise his enthusiasm by taking a lot of casual strolls and to create the illusion of restraint by always refusing to carry a basket and filling his extra-large shirt, which he just happens to be wearing, instead.

Now he carefully selects from his own collection and places the mushrooms in their appropriate piles, making two new places for several kinds of *Lactarius* and coral mushrooms that he has found. The nice thing about both these mushrooms is that, like the boletes, they are easy to recognize: the corals, because they look very much like coral; the *Lactarius*, because of the milk that oozes from their gills when they are cut. And like the boletes, once they are recognized they are reasonably safe. There are no poisonous corals in the East to speak of—mushrooms, snakes, or heads—but in the Pacific Northwest, eating them has been known to cause upset stomach. In the case of *Lactarius*, the color of the milk, which can be white, blue, yellow, orange, or lilac, is a good clue to its edibility, if not always to identification of the species. Like the *Russula*, its evolutionary cousin, the tastier and meatier *Lactarius* usually has a hot taste when toxic. Knowledgeable mushroom hunters will add a package of sourballs to their standard field equipment so they can take a small bite of an unidentified *Lactarius*, spit it out, and, if the aftertaste is bitter, counter it by sucking on a piece of candy.

"But here," says Victor, "is the catch of the day." He goes outside and returns with his tennis racket covered with a magnificent array of chestnut-capped boletes in perfect condition, their pale pink pores firm, their thick, white, slightly tomentose stipes solid enough to walk on. Not a sign of life or decay anywhere, as he shows us proudly. "And I know they're good because they don't stain blue." I look at him sadly, without the heart to speak. For I too have been fooled more than once by this gorgeous mushroom, *Tylopilus felleus*, a bolete that is nontoxic but so vile and acrid in taste that even the slugs reject it, and I have finally learned to recognize this mushroom by the fact that it is permitted to live such a long and healthy life.

"Oh," says Richard almost in a guffaw, "the bitter bolete. I served that in a stew for six last week. There's plenty left over if you want me to go home and get it."

"Never mind." I thank him for the offer.

Victor has moved to the wine rack, and Marie to the stove. "Let's see," murmurs Victor, whose love and appreciation for wines approach my own for mushrooms. "A Montrachet would be nice with the oysters, with the chanterelles, a Pouilly Fuissé." He begins to rearrange the piles of mushrooms according to taste.

Tylopilus felleus

"Let's see," says Marie, who has laid out all the available pots and frying pans on the stove, "we need six more frying pans." She has begun to rearrange Victor's rearrangement.

"How are we going to eat them?" I ask.

"Sautéed, of course. With butter, oil and garlic, and salt and pepper."

"Why don't we just throw them all into a pot and make some nice mushroom barley soup?" asks Jean, who is not Russian.

"What are we going to eat them with?" asks Richard.

"Ducks' eggs," says my son Eric, who has just staggered into the kitchen and had, the day before, been given a dozen ducks' eggs as overtime pay from Dean and DeLuca, the gourmet food shop where he works.

"How about some fresh pheasant?" asks Richard. "I know just where they cross the road, not far from here."

Victor pours us each a glass of wine, and we toast the coming feast. "Look at that," says Richard, "a symphony in orange." And he is right. There before him is a mound of orange mushrooms: the chicken mushroom, *Hypomyces lactifluorum*, the chanterelles, two species of orange *Lactarius—volemus* and *hygrophoroides*—and *Tylopilus ballouii*. "How about some orange juice?" I ask.

Victor pours some more wine, and the smell of sizzling mushrooms begins to drift out the kitchen door. The table is set, and plates of mushrooms, followed by ducks' eggs, nitrate-free bacon, and chunks of Russian pumpernickel follow. We all sit down, and Victor pours us each another glass of wine. "Wait a minute," I say, "what about Michael?" Michael, our second son, who is fourteen, is playing tennis and should be returning soon. "We'll save some for him," says Victor.

It is just noon, and the sun is full in the sky. Dappled shadows fall from the leaves above our heads, onto our arms and necks, onto the table, into the plates of mushrooms and glasses of wine. The feast is finally finished. One by one we leave the table, full of sun, wine, mushrooms, and sleep, stretching out along the grass like strands of filamentous hyphae, interwoven randomly, crisscrossing arms and legs. I am the last to leave the

table, making certain that there is at least one taste of every mushroom for Michael, who is now rounding the driveway on his bike. No longer able to stand, I slide to the soft ground and curl up under a tree, my mission accomplished.

"We saved you some," I call softly to Michael, who approaches the table.

"Mmmm," he says, sniffing from plate to plate, completely ignoring the motionless figures sprawled about him on the lawn. "A lot of mushrooms." He puts down his tennis racket.

"We saved you some," I repeat the phrase weakly.

"I see that," he acknowledges. "Any parasols?"

I shake my head, unable to speak any longer. He is silent for a long moment. "Well, then," he says, "never mind." He picks up his racket and goes into the house. "You know I only eat parasols." And then, afraid that he might seem unappreciative: "But thanks anyway."

CHAPTER 7

The Mushroom Foray: Celebration of the Harvest

In LATE AUGUST, a primitive herding urge strikes the mushroom hunter. During long weekends from August through early November, amateur mycologists from Idaho, Connecticut, Michigan, and Oregon converge on vacant camps, college campuses, and state park facilities to hunt and gather, eat, identify, draw, dry, and discuss mushrooms.

Forays, fairs, and picnics are intense events run by the local, state, regional, and national mushroom societies. Sometimes forays are quiet and intimate events, serious expeditions of twenty people into the wild to collect specimens for study and talk. Other times, up to three hundred people are in attendance, with all the unfocused hullabaloo of a political convention, at a carnival of competing lectures and cooking demonstrations, mushroom display tables, and improvised stands piled high with books, ceramic ashtrays, silkscreened T-shirts, notepaper, jewelry, dishtowels, and belts for sale, all with mushroom motifs.

To the outside world, the diversity of mushroom people, like mushrooms themselves, are difficult to distinguish. Inside the hermetically sealed world of the foray, it is somewhat easier. There are pothunters and taxonomists, painters and photographers, experts in *Tricholoma* and *Inocybe*, cultivators of *Psilocybe*, collectors of *Lycogola*. Sometimes there is competition among the mushroom hunters. Among photographers, the advocates of natural light have contempt for the advocates of flash. Field identifiers and microscope-users look askance at one another. There are scorekeepers and namedroppers. What's the difference between a *Strobilomyces floccopus* and a *Strobilomyces confusis*? When is an *Entoloma* not an *Entoloma*? (When it's a *Leptonia*, of course.)

The slide-show lecture is a fundamental ritual at every mushroom foray. From the darkened auditorium, professional mycologists and chosen amateurs promise to lead their followers into enlightenment: "An Introduction to the Genus *Cortinarius*"; "The Cultivation of Mushrooms Wild and Tame"; "Tricky *Tricholomas*"; "Bolete Spores as Seen Through a Scanning Electron Microscope"; "Hunting for Hallucinogens"; "How to Dry, Pickle, and Preserve Mushrooms"; "The Natural History of the Lichen"; "Spore Dispersal in the Basidiomycetes"; "Atta, the Fungus Growing Ant"; "Discomycetes"; "Some Highlights and Sidelights of *Lactarius*".

Expectant, I lean forward in my chair, eager to learn something about the symbiotic mycorrhizal relationship between fungi and trees, the procedure of parasitism, the life cycle of slime molds, the chemistry of toxins, and phylogeny and ontogeny. What is the meaning of color in mushrooms? What makes a genus a genus? How does the morphological structure of a mushroom contribute to its survival? The world of mushrooms is infinite. Mushroom people are insatiable.

Sometimes I am charmed by anecdotes, provoked and satisfied, moved by moments of understanding and glimpses into a world inside a world. In sixty minutes, eighty to a hundred species march across the screen like soldiers on review. There must be something in their genes or early childhood training, for no matter where they start, most mycological speakers wind up giving taxonomic travelogues: *Polyporus albellus, Panellus stipticus, Russulae aeruginea, chameolenta,* and *cyanoxantha, Sepedonium chrysospermum,* or *Phylloporus rhodoxanthus.* I sink slightly into my chair and wonder if a shepherd tells his flock apart so well? How long would it take the expert standing in front of the room to learn the names of his hundred rapt listeners?

Professional mycologists are never satisfied. *Polyporus berkeleyi* is now *Bondarzewia berkeleyi,* and *Polyporus sulphureus* has become *Laetiporus sulphureus. Pholiotae* have been removed from the family Cortinariacae, and many *Lepiotae* are no longer simply *Lepiotae.* The endless stream of name changes brings a groan from the audience. I sink even further down into my seat, wondering when science is going to catch up with the Church and translate all this Latin into the vernacular.

"It's all nonsense, all of it," declares Bud Schwartz, a veteran amateur mycologist and photographer and a retired manufacturer of precision optical equipment. "I don't care a damn for all those names. It's the beauty of nature that gets me excited. The beauty and the wonder and the mystery. Just wait," he assures me, "for my slide show on *Pilobolus.* You'll see how simple it all is."

Pilobolus is Greek for "hat-thrower," and a most appropriate name it is for this tiny mushroom. Rarely larger than an eighth of an inch high, the *Pilobolus crystallinus* is a marvel of engineering and a bundle of energy, with enough turbopressure buildup to send a spore flying six feet. For a five-foot-eight-inch man like Bud Schwartz to display strength proportional to this mushroom's, he would have to hurl his hat three-quarters of a mile!

"A few years ago, in Litchfield, Connecticut," he continues, "I saw a ball of horse dung that looked as though it were covered with frost. Inspecting it more closely, I was shocked to see that this frost was really composed of hundreds of thousands of tiny fungi. They were all leaning over"—and Bud Schwartz tilts the upper half of his body to demonstrate—"aimed in the same direction. I found out later that *Pilobolus* is light sensitive, or phototropic. All of them," he says twice, in wonderment that is catching, "in perfect symmetry, leaning toward the light. It's almost too beautiful to describe."

Dung! I think to myself as Bud Schwartz shows us his homemade laboratory and dung garden. *There is too much of it in the world already.* His garden consists of moistened plates covered with bell jars, under which he has placed the dung of rabbits, mice, cows, horses, and deer. Now he is planning to start work with geese and has discovered that the aquatic-grazing moose will not do because *Pilobolus*, which germinates on grass, grows only on the dung of terrestrial herbivores. But what reasonable person, I wonder, can afford to be seen crawling along the ground in search of droppings from rabbit and deer?

In a closeup magnification, a forest of tiny, clear jewels flashes on the screen. Wearing black hats called sporangia, they all lean in unison toward the light. When the pressure builds up inside the stipe and subsporangial layer, the black hat goes flying and the spores are ejected into the air. *Pilobolus* leans toward the light, we are told, so that the spore mass is less likely to land on a rock, tree, or building. It aims its spores to land on the grass, where they can be eaten by an animal, pass through the animal's system, and keep the life cycle going. To ensure their survival, a mucilage, or gluelike substance, called cell sap adheres the spores to their landing surface. And there the spores wait, sometimes for up to a year, until the right horse or rabbit comes along to graze on the grass. "What would *Pilobolus* do," asks someone from the back of the room, "if you tried to deceive it by throwing light from all directions?" Without hesitation, Bud Schwartz answers quietly: "Go mad!"

This is a multimedia display in miniature: the world of the small is always full of secrets and surprises. *Ping, Ping,* pingpingping, an ear pressed against the bell jar at around one o'clock hears the sound of shooting spores. A Cook's tour of Bud Schwartz's greenhouse dung garden appears on the screen, with even rows of plates, jars, and metal pots. "See how simple it is," says the gardener. "All you need is some crushed dung balls, blotting paper, a plate, and something to keep in the humidity." Yes, of course, and a bellows, extension tubes, and a reversed macrolens, not to mention a microscope and the seventeen-piece invention called the Budget (Bud's gadget). The Budget includes clamps, clips, tubes, forceps, and a small mirror, all to make the photographing of a small object a little easier. The camera moves in on *Pilobolus* at all its stages: the crystal droplets forming on the side of the stipe as the pressure mounts; the pigment carotin at the base of the subsporangial swelling; the elfin black forest moving toward the light like MacDuff's soldiers toward Dunsinane.

"Let's say I'm a *Pilobolus*," the Brobdingnagian Bud Schwartz suggests, as if we didn't already think he was. Twisting his upper back to demonstrate, he raises his arms in a *port de bras*, lifts the black beret from his head, and hurls it clear to the back of the room. That is all you know on earth and all you need to know.

At the end, he holds up a plastic bag containing some dried deer dung. "Who wants to try?" he asks. "It's really quite simple. All you need is—" From the last row comes a voice, "Me! Me! Over here!" I am waving wildly and reaching for the bag before I am even aware that the voice is my own.

This slide show, educational and sometimes entertaining, is only one of many foray sideshows. There are classes in photography and workshops in mycophagy, sometimes a visit to a commercial mushroom-growing plant, a demonstration in spore-print art, and mushroom silkscreening. Outside, Bunji Tagawa, regarded by many as the best mushroom illustrator in the country, is painting watercolors, explaining to the gathered crowd that there is green in the brown cap and blue in the white gills. There are always people on their stomachs photographing mushrooms, and people on their stomachs photographing other people on their stomachs. Inside, a young woman sits motionless in a corner, peering through a microscope.

But the main event is the foray itself—the communal hunt. Inside the large hall, everything has been readied for the celebration. Miles of tables are set up to display the bounty. Attending mycologists await the hunters' offerings. Sorters, foray leaders, and official recorders await their tasks. Advance scouts have staked out the hunting grounds. Frying pans and campstoves stand patiently in the corner.

It is nine in the morning, and the procession of seven or eight cars moves somberly down the road like a funeral cortege. A large sign, FORAY #1, is set in the front window of the lead car. At the site, the groups split up and spread out. Each foray leader has already described the terrain and has admonished those in his charge not to get lost, giving a short survival lecture in case they do. (More often than not, someone does, and more often than not, it is me. I have been lost with people who made the hours seem like minutes and vice versa, and with survivors who kept the sun over their left shoulder, who recalled which way the streams were running, and who knew that deer tracks meant grass and civilization ahead. But I have never been lost with anyone who remembered to take a compass.)

Among mushroom people, hunting styles and methods vary widely. Some hunters stalk only large crops of edibles, while others crouch at the edges of creeks, poking in the moss and peering through a hand lens at tiny twig-dwelling *Marasmii* and *Mycenae*. Cautious hunters stick to the soft needle beds of conifer woods, where masses of boletes and *Suilli* sit right out in the open and where multicolored leaves and poison ivy do not confuse the senses and contaminate the sensitive. But the greatest diversity of prey is found in the mixed hardwood and conifer forests that are unique to two areas in the world, according to Dr. Sam Mazzer, a botany professor at Kent State University. He describes the mycological affinities between the eastern United States and temperate East Asia: "There are more species of trees right here in Connecticut [or Carroll County, Ohio, depending on where he is speaking, as long as it is east of the Mississippi] than in all of Europe and the Pacific Northwest." That makes all of us Easterners feel better about feeling constantly diminished by the epic vistas and abundance of mushrooms in the Douglas fir and aspen forests of the Rockies and the Far West.

"Why are there more species?" he tantalizes. Before the Ice Age, the area from Ohio to Connecticut was tropical and subtropical forest and the more temperate zones extended up to the arctic regions. When the last glaciation crept down across Siberia and Canada, most of the land mass to the south remained intact, providing a habitat suitable for the wide variety of flora and fauna that now inhabit it. As the ice receded, the temperate forests simply moved north. In Europe, however, the Alpine and Scandinavian glaciers met, crushing between them the mixed forests, thereby limiting the number of species that could dwell there. In California and the Far West, the land mass has been rising, sending up new mountains and changing the climate. The pattern of cold dry winters and warm wet summers reversed, affecting the flora and turning the temperate mixed woods into single-species forests.

Some mushroom hunters are gregarious amblers, engrossed in conversation, stopping to look at vines and wildflowers as well as mushrooms. Others are pure and singleminded, solitary hunters who forage on the fringes. There are those who pick up everything they see and ask "What's this? What's this?" And there are those who always know the answer.

On this particular foray, I am only interested in *Pilobolus*. In order to reach the woods, we must cross a cow pasture. I move methodically from cow flop to cow flop on my hands and knees, peering through a hand lens. All kinds of interesting things are growing out of the dung, but no *Pilobolus*. "Find anything?" A small group that has seen me stop comes running. "Only dung," I answer. They continue on into the woods. Most dung hunters are college students from the Universities of Washington, Louisiana, and Florida who scour the dairy farms looking for the hallucinogenic *Psilocybe* and *Panaeolus*. One member of the group lingers behind. "Won't find 'em here," he assures me. "I'm not looking for 'em,"

I assure him in return. "What are you looking for?" "*Pilobolus,*" I answer. "What's that?" "A beautiful tiny white mushroom," I begin to explain. "Does it get you high?" he asks. "Some people," I answer.

As the day moves along, the hunters drift back to camp. Their baskets are overflowing with *Russulae* and *Lactarii,* blewits and boletes, puffballs and polypores. Not far from the display table is a sorting area, where able hands help foragers sift through the specimens, separating species and discarding excess twigs, needles, and poison ivy leaves. The mushrooms are then placed on paper plates and brought before the presiding mycologists, who accept the offerings and perform the identification rites. At tables that sometimes resemble altars and at other times checkout counters, the faithful line up and the chanting begins: *Russula brevipes, Pseudocolus schellenbergal, Hygrophorus eburneus,* variety *unicolor, ad astra per aspera, Te deum.* . . .

The laying on of names is an old and complex ritual uttered in Latin and administered by those who descend from an ancient apostolic tradition. What's in a name, anyway? A genus and a species, thanks to the eighteenth-century Swedish botanist Carolus Linnaeus, whose precise and compulsive mind brought order and dignity to the biological kingdom; he introduced the system of binomial nomenclature and produced a revolution in the art of scientific name-calling.

Before Linnaeus, there was chaos. From Greek and Roman times until the middle of the eighteenth century, mushrooms were named with far more rhyme than reason, and often divided into simple convenient groupings like *Fungi Esculenti* and *Fungi Noxii et Perniciosi.* Even as knowledge advanced, as the herbalists and scholars of the sixteenth and seventeenth centuries described, identified, and studied fungi, it seemed that there were more names and more schemes for classification than there were mushrooms. Sometimes it was a single word like *Boletus* for *Amanita caesaria;* sometimes a longer, more challenging phrase like *boletus veninus, diluto rubore, rancido, aspectu, livido intus colore, rimosa stria, pallado per ambitum labro*, for none other than *Amanita muscaria*.

When it came to mushroom classification, the geniuses of genus appeared at the start of the nineteenth century: first, South African Christian Hendrik Persoon (1761–1837), followed thirty years later by Elias Fries (1794–1878), a fellow countryman of Linnaeus. Recognized as the joint fathers of mycology, Persoon left his mark on the taxonomy of rusts, smuts, and other microfungi, while Fries sired the system of mushroom taxonomy that is still largely in use today.

After Fries's death, mycologists became so plentiful, inventing names and descriptions of fungi in so many languages, that a new tower of botanical Babel threatened to collapse under the weight of confusion. In 1905 at Vienna, an International Botanical Congress was called to create some semblance of order and to establish the rules of nomenclature. It was there, in the interest of order, that Fries was exalted and his epic work, the *Systema Mycologicum*, was declared the "bible of mycology."

But like most theologies, the Friesian system of classification has suffered a continuous assault on its orthodoxy at the hands of evolutionists. To those who seek the truth in natural affinities and phylogenetic sequences, the Friesian taxa, based on spore color and the observable characteristics of cap, gills, or stipe, may facilitate identification in the field, but in today's world of microscopic connections, it seems artificial and self-limiting: a neat catalogue of species that soothes the orderly mind but eludes the deeper spirit.

Today's professional mycologists, including those who

attend the amateur forays, are usually state university teachers of botany and mycology with a special interest in the taxonomy of large fleshy fungi. More often than not, they are male and Anglo-Saxon with a strong predilection for trout fishing and travel. Many have published scientific monographs describing one genus or more, and all but a few support their studies in mycology either by teaching classes in other, more popular aspects of botany or by receiving grants from government and industry to study crop diseases, paint blisters, strip mining, improving strains of commercial mushrooms, and other subjects of far greater interest to their benefactors than to themselves.

In the scientific world, professional mycologists are the bit players while astrophysicists and microbiologists are the superstars. As a science, at least in this country, the study of fungi still receives some of the contempt that fungi themselves have suffered over the centuries. Even on the one-celled level, they have never achieved the status of the bacteria and the virus. (*E. coli*, the intestinal bacterium that has risen to prominence through gene-splicing, has recently attracted worldwide attention, but who has ever heard of *Neurospora*?) Taxonomists of large fleshy fungi must fight even harder against the scientific currents than other mycologists. They are field people in a world where laboratory cultures have rendered tree stumps obsolete, inhabitants of a micro-universe in which anything you can see with the naked eye or a light microscope isn't worth the paper a grant is printed on. Still, they persist, trying to fit together the pieces of a part of nature's puzzle that everyone else has long since abandoned. Unlike Columbus and Balboa, Shakespeare and Galileo, their successes are not blockbusters; but their drive is the same—to make sense of the world and order of the universe.

To the amateur, the mycologist is a hero and demigod, sorcerer and soothsayer, who brings to the foray an air of authority and to the obsession an air of responsibility. To the professional, the amateur is an ardent, sometimes tiresome proselyte whose votive offerings are viewed as fair exchange for instructing the uninitiated into the mysteries of nomenclature and identification. To forage in Texas, California, Michigan, North Carolina, and Connecticut over the course of a single summer and fall, to see three hundred collections over a single weekend, to find six specimens that puzzle them and three amateurs that interest them, the professionals are willing to sit still for several hours at a time, naming a hundred species for the hundredth time and answering the question "But can you eat it?" for the two hundredth time.

In the beginning, spirits are high. Every devotee and every mushroom gets equal attention. "What's this? And this? And this?" The faithful crowd gathers around. "There's our old friend *Laccaria laccata*." I thought so, we mumble, and lower our heads in shame for having missed the obvious. We have seen it a thousand times.

"Come on now, you know what this one is. Just look at those fibrils on the cap." His trusting eyes are for me alone. I can't let him down. *"Inocybe fastigiata,"* I sputter.

"I'll have to scope this one later." He peers at the gills through a hand lens. A smile of pride. We handed him a hard one.

Bearers carry the baptized to their appropriate sections: ASCOMYCETES, POLYPORES, LACTARIUS, TREMELLA, all marked in bold black letters, as a scribe or recorder—sometimes the wife (rarely the husband) of an attending mycologist, sometimes an honored amateur—carefully inscribes in a book the genus and the species of every mushroom identified.

The number of species named at a national foray is usually between two and three hundred. In 1974 in North Carolina, an extraordinary five hundred species were collected. Word spread like wildfire among the foragers in the countryside, where all-night revelry and celebration followed. Plans were hatched by the elders to return to the same location in 1980, but only a paltry three hundred came in that year.

The great hall fills with people. Alone and in twos, they pace the aisles back and forth beside the display tables, sometimes deep into the night when the room is kept open. "Oh, yes, that used to be a . . . I can't keep these names straight." We pick up mushrooms and turn them over, taking notes and photographs as we try to learn. "How on earth did he tell these two apart?" Brilliant colors and mushroom aromas blur in the late afternoon.

The energy level drops. Mushrooms shrivel before we even get a chance to look at them. Plates of mixed species begin to appear. Mushrooms begin to disappear, to be photographed, to be eaten, to go home with the professionals to be studied. The sorters cannot sort fast enough, and everyone is out of sorts. Piles of mushrooms lie waiting, unnamed, unattended. Someone asks, "But can you eat it?" for the two hundred and first time.

And then it is over, almost before it began. Fallen from grace, the mushrooms are swept from the tables into giant bins. *Clitocybes, Tricholomae, Clavariae*—all intermingle and are forgotten. The professionals and the serious taxonomists among the amateurs forage through the last leftovers, while the rest of us pack our bags and baskets with five new names (three people and two mushrooms). Eventually, the last foray of the year must end, and we are on our way home to familiar tastes and territories. The season will soon be over.

But for the Westerner and the handful of itinerant hunters, it is only beginning. Microscope and camera in hand, field guides on their backs, they are off to Seattle and the Olympic Peninsula, to Portland and Idaho and Houston. As the wolf follows the caribou across the tundra, and as the golf pro follows the touring circuit, the mushroom hunter follows the foray, here, there, everywhere. But the rest of us must wait for spring, when a new cycle of life begins.

CHAPTER 8

Spore Trek

ON CLOSER INSPECTION, the young woman at the foray who peers so intently into the microscope is not so young after all; and she is me. My head is bowed, eyes fastened to the binocular eyepieces. I am peering at an *Inocybe* gill section, measuring spores with my freshly calibrated micrometer and scrutinizing cystidia for their size, shape, and precise location along the edge and face of the gill.

An *Inocybe* is one of the small, innocuous-looking varieties of gilled mushrooms that proliferate in field and forest, moss and dung, grass and showers, with great profusion and little distinction. The mushrooms of the genus *Inocybe* are known in the mushroom trade as LBMs, or little brown mushrooms, and share that honor with a dozen other genera and hundreds of species spread far and wide. *Agrocybes* and *Conocybes, Psathyrellae* and *Tuberiae, Hebelomae* and *Galerinae,* the color of their caps and spore prints are generally some shade of brown; they range in shape from convex to umbrellalike; in size from half an inch to two inches. They are difficult to tell

Inocybe

apart, and many are toxic. Were it not for the deadly toxic *Galerina* and the hallucinogenic varieties of *Psilocybe*, *Panaeolus*, and *Stropharia*, little brown mushrooms would go unnoticed forever, stepped on and stepped over by all but the most dedicated mycologists.

What distinguishes the *Inocybe* from other little brown mushrooms are primarily the radial fibrils, or hairs, that run along the surface of the umbonate cap, which resembles, I suppose, a small chocolate kiss. Within the borders of the little-brown-mushroom world, the *Inocybe* is a member of the family Cortinariacae, a group of medium-size, middle-of-the-road mushrooms, with medium-brown caps and medium clay-brown gills and spore prints. This genus contains more or less six hundred species, all looking more, rather than less, alike. The *Inocybe* is nothing to write home about. You can't eat it. It is dull and dingy in appearance, often pungent and unpleasant of odor. A hard mushroom to spot, it is not much to look at once you do see it. The *Inocybe* is the essence of insignificance.

Why then am I here, sitting indoors on such a beautiful day, when I could be outside scaling Englemann spruce and aspen slopes, wading through wildflowers in rocky alpine meadows? Why am I staring down into this rabbit hole, drowning in a sea of spores, when I could be out there in the real world sampling *Lepista* Stroganoff or learning about lichens?

There is no science in my genes. What then is the power of this Faustian machine, the microscope, that lures me like a peepshow barker, from the safety of home and hearth, with hints and promises of secrets revealed? What warlock has worked his spell on my soul, willing me to carry forty pounds of optical paraphernalia from airport to airport across the country?

I still do not know a crocodile from an alligator, a fir from a spruce, a Schubert lied from a Brahms lied. I cannot tell where Orion's belt begins and ends in the northern sky. There was a time when I would have been more than content to know an *Amanita* from a *Lepiota*, a *Clavaria* from a *Ramaria*. There was more than enough to see in a lifetime with my naked eyes, to grasp with my naked intelligence. Using a microscope seemed somehow to violate the integrity of nature's borders. It was a cheap thrill, a kind of cheating, like looking up the answers in the back of a book.

Why then am I drawn to this poor *Inocybe* gill, this tiny speck of splattered matter, crushed between slide and coverslip in a watery solution of potassium hydroxide? I have always wanted to know something that no one else I know knows, to carve out a niche of obscurity and die before my task is complete. I would pursue success relentlessly, only to despair at its approach; I would choose one intimate friend over twenty-five acquaintances. There are mushrooms we come to know by sight and smell, by touch and taste. *Inocybes* and other small brown mushrooms we can only know by penetration.

Dozens of brown bottles are dripping with colorful chemicals. Razors and tweezers, slides and coverslips, books and monographs lie askew, spilling across the workspace. I am where I belong, shielded by a fortress of science, enveloped in a gentle glow of alchemy, safely removed from the combat zone. "Here, take a look at these. See what you can make of them." It is the peripatetic proprieter of this portable mycological laboratory, Gary Lincoff, midway between forays, home from the Polypore Wars just long enough to dump a pile of mushrooms in my lap. Before I can say *Pluteus flavorfuligineus*, he will be, like the White Rabbit, off again.

Dashing from table to table, he is gathering fresh edibles for his mycophagy workshop in the afternoon and picking from among the more esoteric specimens to help identify the unidentified, confirm correct identities, and correct mistaken identities. Holding up slides to the light, he is preparing his lecture for the evening on toxic mushrooms. President of NAMA, the North American Mycological Association, he is halted at every bend by questions about next year's foray, complaints about last year's, and invitations by local club presidents to talk in Ohio, Washington, California. A serious amateur (he makes his living teaching and writing about mushrooms although he has no degree in mycology) whose appetites for knowledge and food are equally insatiable, there are few things he enjoys more than talking and very little in his life that doesn't involve mushrooms.

I was surprised to learn that he saw his first mushroom as recently as 1971 and not at all surprised that his obsession—like that of many mushroom hunters—grew out of a series of other obsessions. A protest-scarred veteran of the mid-sixties, Gary began writing a novel about a draft evader surviving in Central Park. To learn if survival were possible, he set about learning every botanical species in the city's dozen parks. Eventually, the novel faded away and the botanical information led to economic survival through walks and workshops on edible wild foods.

One day he found a mushroom in Riverside Park, bought a field guide, keyed it out as *Coprinus micaceus,* or inky cap, and saved it in his freezer. The following week, he took the mushroom to an amateur mycologist to be positively identified. It was a hot July day, and by the time he got there the mushrooms had dissolved into black mush. "Oh yes," said the identifier without a second glance, "that looks just like an inky cap to me."

"Pileus fleshy, putrescent, subconic at first"—I am holding a specimen in one hand and flipping through the *Inocybe* key in the other—"then campanulate to subexpanded, innately silky, fibrillose or fibrillose-squamulose, dry or rarely viscid." Written in 1918, this is the only published key on American *Inocybes.* It contains about a hundred species of the eight hundred known to exist. Up to here, everything checks out with the genus *Inocybe.* As for the rest of the description—"spores angular or even, the epispore tuberculate, spiny or smooth; apical pore absent; cystidia present or absent"—I will have to turn to the microscope for verification.

A mushroom spore is enormously varied. It is a single cell, made up of a cell wall, protoplasm, and a nucleus. Spores range in size from 2 to 150 microns. (A micron is 10^{-6} or $1/1,000,000$ of a meter.) Their shapes are globose and ellipsoid, ovoid and oblong, cylindrical and fusiform, nodulose and angular. Their surfaces are smooth and bumpy, decorated with warts and grooves, ridges and reticulations. Some spores have thick walls, others thin. On some, there is a tiny opening at one end called a germ pore; on others, a smooth, sandy oasis, or plage, amidst the rocky shore.

Once the microscope replaced field intelligence as the major taxonomic weapon, spores, as the basic units of reproduction, became the basic factor on the generic battleground. Genera were redefined and realigned by spore shapes and ornamentation. This new knowledge stirred insurrections and secessions from tribes that had become too unwieldy to control. Among the gilled mushrooms, *Lyophyllum*, *Melanoleuca*, and *Galerina* won their independence from the large colonial powers *Tricholoma*, *Clitocybe*, and *Pholiota*. The balkanization of the hard woody bracket fungi, once united under the genus *Polyporus*, into *Bondarzewia*, *Ganoderma*, and *Bolitopsis* due to microscopic features has caused no end of mycological crossfire.

What's in a genus anyway, but a cellblock in which prisoners are placed for efficient management? I read somewhere that "science packs its theoretical suitcase with a sock hanging out here, a shirttail there. So long as it can be closed, after a while no one notices tag ends of things that won't pack." I remember when I was a child, my mother, who directed a summer camp for girls, fiddled each May with tags of paper and a photograph album. Fascinated, I would watch her hands move like a magician's, placing and replacing the white tags (each representing a camper), five on a page (each representing the side of a bunk). "Linda's a little younger," she would muse, "but rather mature." "No, I can't put those two together again. Irene's mother thinks that Lois is a bad influence." Now, my mother was someone who knew what a genus is.

Under the scope, my spores are brown and bumpy. A school of crippled starfish swim into view, radiating four, five, six points, blunt at the edges, irregular. I roam from spore to spore, increasing the power and fiddling with the fine focus, just to make certain. I am elated. The angular spores tell me my specimen can't be anything but an *Inocybe*, something, of course, that I already knew.

"What are you looking at so intently?" a passerby stops to ask.

"*Inocybe* spores. Would you like to see?"

"Anything special about them?"

"Not really," I answer.

"Then why would I want to look at them?"

Behind me, Aaron Noraravian is waiting patiently to use the scope. He is looking for hyphal clamp connections, those special hooklike structures that form during nuclear division, connecting two segments of hyphae as they split into daughter cells. In a field where color is paramount in identification, Noraravian, who is color blind, makes up in exactitude for what he lacks in chromatic perception.

"Mind if I have a look?" he asks. I remove my slide to make room for his clamp connections, but it is my *Inocybe* he wants to look at. "Nice spores," he says. I'm flattered. "Angular," he confirms. "An *Inocybe*. Have you got any more information?"

I tell him I'm working on it, and while he is looking for clamp connections I flip through the key with trepidation. Finding the spores and identifying the genus are only the start of the journey. A seeker of species is like the lone Marlow chugging up the silent, treacherous river after Kurtz in Conrad's *Heart of Darkness*. The murky liquid holds many secrets. Millions of spores swim around me. A tangled web of filamentous hyphae passes through the hazardous pileus. To find the species is to run aground, smacking into the sharp gill edges and giant cystidia that line the hymenial shores.

The species, they say, is the only natural order in the world, because it is interfertile. All other groupings are man-made. "But we don't really know what they do down there under the ground, now do we?" is an admission that has been made publicly by one mycologist and privately by most others. After all, courtship rituals among mushrooms are rarely observed, and while mushroom hunters often do stumble across woodland copulations, they are far more likely to be among king snakes or woodcocks than among chanterelles or puffballs. Lab cultures tell the tale, of course, but out of thousands and thousands of species, only a small percentage of mushroom mycelia have been successfully observed mating.

I often feel like a voyeur, invading nature's privacy. Why are we human beings so driven to see what we cannot, to know what we do not? If God had meant for us to see the whole universe, he would have given us the eyes to do so. But then he did give us the brains to create our own visions, to invent new "eyes" like microscopes and chromotography. Is he tempting us? Is he himself ambivalent, anxious to absolve himself of responsibility? Perhaps he understands the human nature that he himself created so well that he knows that we will be sure to look at that which is hidden. Maybe, on the other hand, it is the devil at work.

One summer day, I went for a walk with my son Michael, who was then very young. We came upon a black cherry tree that was infected by a giant gall fungus. Michael pulled at me; "Let's go," he said. "There's nothing to be afraid of," I explained. "It's not a wasps' nest or anything like that, only a growth on a tree." He was cold. "That's nature's business," he said, "not yours." Turning on his heels, he walked away.

We are all voyeurs, peeking at the sky through our telescopes, feeling the pulse of the earth with our Geiger counters, observing the courtship and mating rituals of animals with ethological detachment, searching for the origins of life.

How then do we identify a mushroom species? With the larger and more colorful mushrooms, we can often trust our naked eyes. The fleshy fungi of the field have the color of their caps for us to go by. When that is too variable, there is the gill attachment. When that varies too much, there is always the shape of the cap, the texture of the stipe, the base, the presence or absence of an annulus, the habitat. When we can no longer trust our unadorned vision, the microscope becomes a tool for truth. Machines don't lie or make mistakes, and once we learn how to use them, they don't confuse us. Once we know the genus, all we have to do is measure the spores, locate and measure the cystidia, find the clamp connections, and determine whether the cuticle is an ixotricodermium. A drop or two of Meltzer's reagent will tell us whether we have an *Amanita flavaconia* or *frostiana*. KOH will turn the cystidia of *Stropharia rugoso-annulata* the color of spun gold.

I am anxious to move on in the quest for knowledge. My *Inocybe* spores are definitely angular, but the key that I have for reference, I am learning rapidly, has simply opened and closed one small door, leaving me standing in front of a thick concrete wall. Angular spores, I am reading, can also be tuberculate and spiny, or they can be simply angular-tuberculate. Those that are tuberculate and spiny can be nodulose or not nodulose. Those that are angular or angular-tuberculate can also be not truly angular or unevenly angular. How, I wonder, could I, who have been through the Hundred Years' War and the forty-two Beethoven sonatas, to hell and back with Dante, Milton, and George Bernard Shaw, how could I have missed the subtleties and nuances embodied in the angular spores of the *Inocybe*?

For a spore to be measured accurately, it should ideally come from a spore print rather than from the edge

of a gill, where it would not yet have matured sufficiently to be released. The specimens here are too fresh
for prints, and I don't have all day. To locate cystidia, on
the other hand, those large, sterile, somewhat ambiguous
cells that often line the face and edge of a gill, a perfect,
neat, razor-thin, longitudinal cross-section from the gill
is required; this is an enterprise which I have been un-
successfully trying to master for two years.

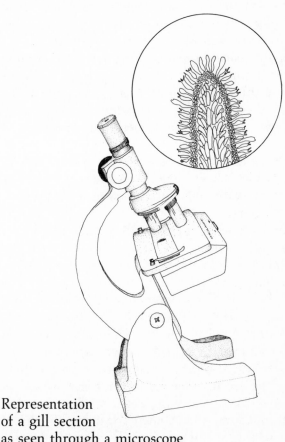

Representation
of a gill section
as seen through a microscope

The gill is a masterpiece of engineering. Hyphal canals and roadways connect the interior to the outside. Dense forests of spore-bearing basidia line the edges, interspersed every so often with large cystidia, jutting out like promontories into the sea. The function of cystidia is but one of the many mycological mysteries that are still unsolved. Large, sterile cells on the face and edges of the gill, they are thought by some to aid in water retention, the mushroom's most precious and difficult-to-come-by means of survival. The gill, designed to hold the greatest number of spores to the smallest surface area, has perhaps sacrificed in water retention capacity what it gained in spore-bearing capacity. The cystidia, standing like windbreaks among that basidia, might baffle the air and function as humidifiers as well, creating channels inside the gill to enhance the movement of water. They are also believed to aid in the dispersal of the spores in that they hold the gills apart and give the spores more room to drop; and they act as excretory agents for the mushroom. Some believe that they exude an odor that repels certain predators who attack before the spores are ready to be spread.

From the top down, a perfect gill section will reveal not only the gill but also a tidy stratification of the entire mushroom, including the cuticle and context of the pileus, or cap, and the flesh of the fruiting body. My sections always looks like hall closets that are badly in need of cleaning. They fall on their backs, legs in the air. I lose them in the liquid mount and end up focused on a speck of dust, an eyelash, a broken coverslip, spilled coffee, or once, believe it or not, a tree outside my window. But my sections are usually cut so thick that even at a hundred power I am still looking at the murky, seaweed-filled bottom of a swamp. "Thinner, Ed, thinner," I heard the teacher yelling at another equally inept student in

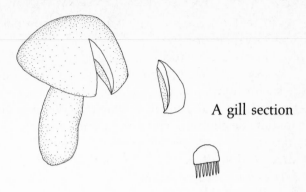

A gill section

the class. "If I want a salami sandwich, I'll go to a deli-catessen."

I cut a new section and put it under the scope, but the view barely improves. Everything is upside down and backward. I cannot tell longitudinal from latitudinal or transverse from transvestite, and I cannot decipher a gill section any better than I can read an architectural rendering or a roadmap. To measure spores, which are smooth and elliptical, is arduous enough; my severely disabled right brain can never keep straight what to instruct my left hand to do, and as soon as I have successfully captured the spore inside the calibrated lines to measure its length, it swims out of sight before I can turn it around. I am slipping and sliding between the slip and the slide, wondering in despair how I will ever measure an angular spore.

I know there is nothing disgraceful about my failure as a section maker, that my verbal skills are probably secretly admired by some brilliant mathematician somewhere. I know that sculptors often turn to fabricators to construct their pieces, that scientists rely on lab technicians to prepare their experiments. But there is something about the frustration as well as the challenge, about learning to develop a new skill, about doing it myself, about making connections, that makes me doggedly, if foolishly, relentless.

I do not climb rocks or hang glide, but I have flown nine thousand feet up and two thousand miles west merely to sit for hours in a dusty classroom surrounded by shattered slides and fungal fragments. While other people are outside climbing rocks and hunting mushrooms, I am staring down the barrel of a microscope, cutting section after section of a *Stropharia johnsoniana* in an unsuccessful attempt to distinguish its filamentous cuticle from its cellular subhymenium. I have learned from the masters how to make a proper section; like stewardesses at takeoff, they stand at the front of the room and explain over and over again the procedure. I listen with rapt attention, absolutely certain that when the time comes, they will find me gasping for air, the oxygen mask wrapped around my ear.

"Carrots, potatoes, elderberry pith if you can get it. Any one of these will work as a cutting board for your gill sections. It's quite a delicate operation, but with a little practice not difficult at all," says University of Michigan Professor Alexander Smith, the most noted mycologist of our day, the prolific author of numerous monographs and popular field guides, and a man with fifty-six years of practice. "Just hack away," advises California mycologist and former Smith student Harry Theirs with an assuring smile, "don't worry about all those fancy techniques for making gill sections." The man on my left suggests that I place the specimen between two slides and make a sandwich. The woman on my right shows me her battle-scarred thumb. "There's no other way," she says.

Noraravian has come and gone with ten clamp connections, lunch has come and gone, the afternoon foray has gone, and I am alone with my *Inocybe* gill and, finally, a section that is clear and sharp. Basidia and cystidia leap out at me. I manage to release and measure a handful of spores. Then, increasing the power, I bear down on the clusters of club-shaped cystidia. Now all I need to do is describe their shape, measure them, and determine their location. On the face of the gill, they are called pleuro-cystidia; on the edge, cheilocystidia. Nothing to it.

Turning to a monograph describing cystidial types, I begin to read, checking out the possibilities: "Cystidia take three basic shapes, Filiform, Cylindrical, and Sub-ventricose." Not bad for a start. "The apex," it continues, "may be Obtuse, Acute or Elongate." I check out my cystidia. Most likely obtuse. Continuing, I read: "Obtuse apices may be divided into the following types: Claviform, Cylindro-Clavate, Clavate, Sphaeropeduncu-late, Napiform." My face presses against the glass, seeking a world I can never enter.

Gary Lincoff has returned from one of his whirlwind tours of the front. Like a harassed waiter, he is precari-ously balancing a pile of paper plates under his chin and along the underside of his forearm. "Look at that—he gestures at a large woody polypore cradled in the crook of his elbow—"that's not a *Ganoderma applanatum*, is it?" "Of course not," I answer.

Clearing a space on the table, I move away from the line of fire. Gary's hands are moving as swiftly as my mother's did playing with her tags, as expertly as Alex-ander Smith's did playing with his pith sticks. His right and left brain seem to jump cables as one eye peers into the private world of the microscope and the other onto an index card, where he draws and records what he sees. Slicing a section of gill here, a piece of pileus there, add-ing a drop of Chrysl Blue, he murmurs without lifting his head, "What did you find?"

"An *Inocybe*," I answer.

"Good," he says. "Now, what's the species?" How can he ask such a thing? How can I possibly figure it out for a mushroom that has over six hundred species, five hundred and fifty of which look identical, with only two existing keys, one in French, which I can't read, and the other sixty years old and covering only a hundred species?

"Well," I begin, "it has angular spores."

"Good," he says. "Measure them. And don't forget to check the cystidia," he adds, departing for another mission.

"But," I call out after him, "but Fries never even used the microscope to identify mushrooms." His back is turned. "Linnaeus thought spores were insect eggs. Besides," I implore, my voice fading to a whisper, "Robert Hooke, who invented the microscope, never even *saw* a spore."

He is gone, and I sit there alone, staring interminably down this rabbit hole, dimly aware that there is something ludicrous about it all. Looking for spores and cystidia seems a fruitless and trivial task. And what do we get when we find them? More things to look for. Maybe, it occurs to me, this is what the lure of knowledge is all about. Not the momentary thrill of discovery, but the months and lifetimes of frustration and failure that keep us plodding on through life.

CHAPTER 9

Under the Autumn Leaves

I CANNOT IMAGINE A LIFE without brisk afternoons and lengthening twilights. Men may be men in Texas, and youth golden in southern California, but fall is fall in the Northeast, and life without fall seems incomplete.

Fall is a desperate season. Fall is the hunt and the harvest. It is frenzied preparations for squirrels, hedgehogs, and humans, and mass migrations for thrushes and warblers. Small haypiles of lupine and firewood dry in the sun next to thyme and tarragon. Tomatoes ripen on windowsills.

The growing season is over. Hickory nuts and acorns fall to the forest floor, food for the forager, stored and swallowed or spread and scattered to the winds. Cool rains seep through the soil to hasten the process of decay, aiding the termites and millipedes as their grinding and chewing make room for new life. Marauding mycelia, stuffed to the gills, their long season of labor come to fruition, slow their underground activity. In a tremendous burst, they surge to the surface and spores rain over the earth.

I have never seen so many mushrooms. On mossy banks and riverbanks, mountainsides and roadsides, in lumberyards and graveyards, on lawns and in cow pastures, in white birch groves and white pine stands. From the giant Douglas fir of the Northwest to the mixed mesophytic hardwoods of the Northeast, they cover the continent: *Tricholomae* and *Armillariae, Cortinarii* and *Xylariae,* chickens, hens, and old men of the woods, lavender *Lepistae* and orange *Omphalinae, Hericia* and *Hydna* hanging from the trees and hiding under the leaves. Some are spring mushrooms reawakened after a sound summer sleep; others are as faithful to fall as I am. And of course there are *Russulae.* There is no mushroom season without *Russulae.* Morels? No. There are false morels, but nowhere that I know of are there fall morels.

The road through New England is paved with mushrooms. In Massachusetts, where there was one sad morel last spring, there are now a hundred bright boletes. In Vermont, a friend who is a college professor and a farmer takes me on a tour of his property and shows me whole tree trunks shelved with sulphur mushrooms, oysters spilling from fallen logs like barnacles along a sunken ship. "Take them, they're yours"; he gestures gallantly at six giant puffballs spread across the garden path. They are so wide I cannot get my arms around even one of them. Then he wants to show me his giant bear's head *Hydnum.* "It's a beauty," he says. "You'll never see one larger." Politely, I refuse.

Even on the eastern tip of Long Island, there is autumnal excess, in a modest sort of way. I cannot open my door without tripping on mushrooms. I cannot get from my house to the tennis court without filling two baskets. "I've tried everything to get rid of them, but nothing seems to work," laments a distressed home-owner in the garden column of the local newspaper.

I am stopped in the aisles of the supermarket; friends load down my wagon with mushrooms. "Take these. And these." "I found this tall brown mushroom with a thin stem and kind of umbrella-shaped top right in the middle of my azaleas. What do you think it is?" Friends and neighbors drop by, sometimes even people I have never met before. "They're edible?" someone asks suspi-ciously. "Well, you keep them. I'm allergic to mush-rooms."

Maybe I will stay here another season after all, aban-doning my dream of a large virgin tract in an Adirondack forest. Here, where the landscape is closer to lunar rocks than to the Garden of Eden. Dregs of an ancient glacier, the soil is sandy and porous, and the pine barrens, com-pared with those of New Jersey, are far more barren than pine. What is left of our puny oak woods is thick with a tangled underbrush of catbriar and poison ivy. But along with the houses and people came cultivated lawns and garden mulch, roadsides and riding stables, apple or-chards, nurseries, cemeteries, and a Main Street lined with dying elms. A mutilated habitat, perhaps, but lovely for mushrooms.

Locally, there is little competition for mushrooms from the inhabitants. For many who are summer residents, beaches and bikinied bodies form the boundaries of their interests. Others, who stay through fall, constitute a community with high environmental awareness and long-standing botanical interest but take little note of mushrooms. There are garden clubs and wildflower walks and societies to preserve, improve, or even collect mush-rooms (although the two nearest mushroom societies are on the North Shore of western Long Island, far away as mushrooms go).

I am back in East Hampton for the first time in several weeks. It is a glorious and cloudless day in late September. Conditions for mushrooms are perfect: heavy rains have drenched the Northeast during the last few weeks, followed by three days of bright, warm sunshine. Long Island seems longer today than usual, as all the way from Ronkonkoma I am stopped by first one, then by another, roadside attraction. Clumps and clusters of shaggy manes and inky caps, robust *Agarici*, assorted *Lactarii*, and a single long-stemmed parasol spill across the back seat of the car.

The odors of earth and raw potatoes, radishes and burnt rubber, mingle and drift into the front seat. As I drive at a mushroom hunter's pace, my bumper sticker, I BRAKE FOR MUSHROOMS, serves as a warning to passing motorists. I nibble around the edges of a young chicken mushroom and gaze out the window, back and forth across the road, at tree stumps, lawns, and grassy stretches. Six *Amanitae muscariae* neatly ring a sapling spruce. Brilliant orange to pale yellow, with white-specked caps, they range from tiny buttons to stools big enough for two toads. They pose elegantly, as if for a page in a children's picture book.

Not bad for a two-hour ride, I tell myself. Still, I know that the weekend will not feel right until I find my first honey mushroom. The golden honey, which grows in copious clusters at the base of trees and on buried wood and old decaying stumps, is the quintessential fall mushroom, growing like a weed the world over. To the Italians, *chiodini* is the heavenly host. To the rest of us, the honey, properly cooked, is simply a good, edible, versatile mushroom. It comes in so many different forms that mycologists disagree about whether to divide them into two, five, or twelve new varieties and species. A bountiful harvest, the honey is a hedge against hard times. Some years they don't know when to stop—like a plague of gypsy moths, they cover the trees and worm their way through the bark, and also like gypsy moths, the honey doesn't seem to have a natural predator in this country. At times, after a week or two, there is nothing to do but close my eyes, lock my doors and windows, and stay inside until the pestilence is past.

I stop the car a few yards beyond the driveway of a private estate that is fronted by a huge forested lawn of planted white pine. Large and colorful metal sculptures watch over the opening to the house. Although the low iron rail that borders the property is not much of a deterrent to the determined interloper, the large, bold NO TRESPASSING signs posted every few yards are somewhat more threatening, especially the one that reads, WARNING THIS PROPERTY IS GUARDED BY RADAR.

Lawn hunting, I have already discovered, is a risky and challenging business. Lawn people turn out to be as varied as mushroom people and are as unpredictable as the mushrooms on their lawns are. Asking permission, we are taught, is the best policy, and usually it is; sometimes those with the fiercest dogs are the friendliest people, and sometimes those who mow their lawns with the fiercest regularity are often willing to wait until I've been by. Usually I say that I am doing a scientific study on mushrooms. This makes me a serious student and discourages lawn people from eating the objects of my research. Occasionally, I will introduce a lawn person to the delights of his or her own mushrooms, but always with the caveat to eat only what I say to eat and never to pick anything without consulting me first.

Sometimes, however, not asking is the better part of

valor. I could be turned away for all kinds of reasons: suspicion that I'm only casing the place; fear that I will be poisoned and they will be held responsible; the owner himself likes mushrooms; and once I was told that the mushrooms were being saved for someone else. To ask and be turned away makes it difficult to return. Until you are caught, not asking has a certain kind of morally ambiguous innocence. (Neither a birdwatcher nor a deer-hunter, I lack the arrogant assurance of both, who seem to believe that the prey and the property through which it happens to pass belong to everyone.)

The house on this estate is so far back, I'm sure the owner doesn't even know I'm here. He can't like mush-rooms, or there wouldn't be so many left on the grounds. They'll only die anyway, and there will never be a short-age of honeys. In truth, I'm doing him a favor.

If the issue is morally and ethically ambiguous, legally it is perfectly clear, a matter only of assessing the risk-benefit ratio. This is not France, where I might be shot, or even the Catskills, where I already have a police rec-ord for trespassing. So I will take my chances that I won't trigger a land mine and that the radar won't turn out to be the family German shepherd.

I promise myself that I will be quick, and I proceed to negotiate the railing beyond which mushroom paradise awaits. Large *Russulae* and *Lactarii* push up through the pine needles. Boletes. Puffballs. A carpet of corals. A path of honeys leads from tree to tree, all the way to the back of the lawn. My jacket is spread out on the ground, filled with mushrooms. I am thinking about removing my shirt to carry the rest when I look up. Two uniformed men are standing over me; their holsters are just about level with my eyes as I kneel. "Can we help you?" they ask. "Oh, yes," I answer, "I'm so glad you're here." I ex-plain that I'm a neighbor and a student of mushrooms on a research project. I just happened to be driving by and looked everywhere for the owner to ask permission to study his flora. This lawn is a wonderful laboratory, I explain, and these honey mushrooms I am holding just happen to be wonderful to eat as well. I press a large bunch into their arms and instruct them to be sure to cut off the stems, which are tough and fibrous, before cooking them. The tastiest way to eat them, I say, is on pasta. They are also quite good pickled, but they must be thoroughly cooked; raw honeys can cause discomfort.

A little bewildered, they thank me and we exchange names and addresses: I give them mine for that of the owner of the property on which I am trespassing. I tell them I'd be pleased to come and identify the owner's mushrooms for him, if he'd like. Perhaps in exchange he will grant me permission to continue my work. The two guards scoop up the remaining mushrooms into their hats and accompany me to my car.

Some days I feel guilty hunting mushrooms by car. Like chasing polar bears in a helicopter, it seems a cruel and unfair sport. But today, instead of feeling guilty, I am gluttonous. Guilt, I decide, more often comes from having than from wanting. Gluttony, on the other hand, seems to satisfy both need and greed—to have and want at the same time.

Fall fever rages, flushed with the color of turning leaves not yet fallen, inflamed with mushrooms erupting along the surface of the earth. It is hard not to be delirious. Skimhampton Road is blistered with puffballs. Mr. Merlo waves from his window as I approach his house on Old Stone Highway. "Thought you weren't coming back," he calls. "Haven't mowed my lawn in three weeks."

Mr. Merlo's lawn is a paradise: twenty-five to thirty species that I know, dozens that I don't. A huge chicken winds its way up the trunk of an oak. Three *Amanita rubescens* form a neat triangle around a water pipe—their rosy-hued caps identify them unmistakably as blushers. Boletes of many varieties. *Clavariae* and *Ramariae*. A large cauliflower *Sparassis.* And, of course, more honeys. Excited, Mr. Merlo wants to show me his garden. I cannot be rude, but this is no time to admire flowers. But it is not flowers Mr. Merlo points to with pride. For crammed there among the mums and snapdragons is a mass of pale purple blewits. Subtle and delicate in taste and tone, these *Lepistae nudae* are more beautiful to me than all the flowers in the garden. They are a real find as well, for this is the first year I have ever seen them in East Hampton.

I don't mean to be greedy, I think, turning onto Abraham's Path, but where have all the *Lepiotae* gone? Asking mushroom hunters their favorite mushroom is like asking oenophiles their favorite wine or book lovers their favorite book. An unfair question, because anyone so engaged knows that what matters is the texture of the words on the page, the bouquet of the Burgundy in the glass, the glimmer of the golden cap hidden in the grass. It is wine, books, or mushrooms that one loves the most, not Lafite Rothschild '61, *Anna Karenina,* or chanterelles. But if I were forced to select a favorite, it would surely be the *Lepiota procera,* commonly known in the East as the parasol.

Deceptively delicate in appearance, the parasol is a mushroom of substance. There is strength in the slender stem and willfulness in the large round cap, fringed and flared and ringed with disks. Alone or in twos, it grows along the sides of roads, in fields, on lawns, and in open sunny woods.

Although the parasol lacks the hype of the morel and the chanterelle and has never acquired ethnic loyalty, as did the honey and the matsutaki, it has no parallel in taste or texture. Fresh, it holds its firmness. Dried or frozen after light sautéeing, it holds its flavor. (My son Michael munches on dried parasols as if they were potato chips.) Stuffed, or simply broiled with a touch of oil and butter, salt and pepper to taste, it is a cap that cannot be surpassed. Sometimes it is large enough to feed a family of four. Long after the fire is out, long after the rest of the meal is forgotten, the nutty fragrance of the parasol still fills the room and pleases the palate.

For a rank beginner, the parasol is difficult to tell apart from a number of other mushrooms: the *Amanita*, the *Agaricus*, other *Lepiotae—americana, rachodes*—and the green-spored, poisonous *Chlorophyllum molybdites*. For anyone who has played with mushrooms for a year, there is no mistaking it. *Stay away from all mushrooms with white spores, rings, and warted caps*—these warnings ring in our ears. We must learn the difference between scales formed by an expanding cap and patches formed by the remnants of a volva. We must learn to distinguish between a ring that resembles a torn skirt and one that resembles a rolled-down stocking. Once we learn all these things and can tell a swollen base from a volva, and, of course, once we learn to recognize bilateral gill trama and dextranoid spores, our first bite of a parasol will be a triumph. We will know it like the back of our hand. Once I gave four large parasol caps to some friends. "How do you know they're not *Amanitas*?" they asked. "Because," I explained knowledgeably, "they just aren't."

The parasol is versatile. Its large cap provides shelter from thunderstorms for tiny creatures, and serves as their flying carpet and woodland banquet table. Unwilling to be bested, the Californians have dubbed their *Lepiota rachodes* the parasol. Similar in appearance to the *Lepiota procera*, the *rachodes* is not a bad-looking mushroom and not at all bad to eat. But to an Easterner, the only true parasol is his or her own *Lepiota procera*.

I am being greedy. Maybe the parasols have decided to take a rest this season. Maybe they've moved to richer pastures or have become extinct. A new parasol hunter has come into the territory.

But there, directly across the road from where I am standing, are six exquisite parasol mushrooms, strutting like swans across an English garden, their large caps flared, their long necks stretched. The mushrooms, I realize with disappointment, are on Mrs. Jackson's lawn, and her car is in the driveway. Mrs. Jackson is a neighbor who has let me know clearly that she doesn't like me prowling on her property. She has taken my license number and has threatened to call the police, and she orders her kids to mow the lawn whenever they see me coming. I drive on.

There is a large white pine stand out in Northwest Woods that my real estate friend, Clara, has shown me. There I fill my basket with edibles. *Suillus pictus* makes a red and yellow checkerboard across the needled floor. Black and fuzzy-headed, the old-man-of-the-woods, *Strobilomyces floccopus*, has popped up only seconds before I arrive. How many quarts of soup will they make? A red-capped *Leccinum* the size of a table lamp casts a shadow on the ground.

Dabs of purple *Cortinarius* paint the woods. I sit resting on the ground, gazing with reverence into the middle of an old garbage dump, where an *Amanita virosa* stands amidst the broken bottles. How exquisite, I whisper, admiring the silky sheen, pure and white as an angel. Fall, I know, also brings the *Amanita phalloides*, its pale-to-olive-green–brown death cap and its perfectly formed, if somewhat ostentatious, basal sac forcing even the most brazen hunters to keep their distance. Like many colonial Americans, *phalloides* was a stowaway hiding among the roots of imported European trees and shrubs. It was first discovered in New Jersey in 1947 and has since been spreading steadily. It was seen only a year ago on western Long Island. I have never found it here, but since it is already at our doorstep, it can't be long before that arrogant specter arrives here.

And then there are more edibles. My first beefsteak mushroom, *Fistulina hepatica*, looks more like liver than beef, and I can only imagine Phillip Roth's Portnoy finding such an object in his mother's kitchen. Large clumps of bricktops cluster around old stumps—also a first this season. On the way home, I detour in order to pass the Jackson driveway. The car is still there.

At my own house, the table is already piled high with mushrooms from today, yesterday, and the day before. Glasses are all over the house making spore prints. Jean has been by with her usual motley array to be identified; among them are *Amanitae, Russulae, Strophariae rugoso-annulatae*, and a large number of nondescript, indistinguishable, and slightly decayed brownish mushrooms. Richard has dropped off a large paper bag with a note attached: "Found so many of these, I'm sick of them. Thought you might know what to do with them." Honeys, of course.

Victor and Michael walk in. "Just these," says Michael, dumping a large armful of more honeys onto the table, totally obliterating my serious if feeble attempts to create some order. Victor begins to organize the mushrooms, separating the honeys by quality into As, Bs, and Cs. Michael is complaining that there are no glasses left to drink from and that he is afraid to remove one from the table for fear that it might contain deadly *Amanita* spores. I am wandering aimlessly, trying to decide what to do next, or even first: Begin writing descriptions of the unidentified species? Get out the pans and pickling jars? Start cleaning the edibles? Tell Michael to stop complaining? I take out my cookbooks. Quiche, stew, Stroganoff, soup, spaghetti sauce, soufflé, *osso buco*, ratatouille, chicken livers and mushroom, veal and mushroom . . . There are enough mushrooms here to keep a restaurant in business for a year. But I cannot stop thinking about Mrs. Jackson's lawn.

Then, almost without realizing it, I have picked up the car keys and gone out the door. "Where are you going?" Victor calls.

"For a drive," I answer.

CHAPTER 10

The Mushroom Connection

Until recently, few respectable mushroom hunters would intentionally eat hallucinogenic mushrooms. They were drugs, not mushrooms, something you took, not ate, and belonged to another generation. The psychoactive species were barely mentioned in the popular field guides, and when they were, they were buried among the toxic species (those that are truly poisonous).

As a respectable mushroom hunter, I was impatient with the number of young people I met who, upon learning that I hunted mushrooms, invariably asked, "Magic mushrooms?" "All mushrooms are magic," I answered.

But once, I wondered. An intriguing passage in an old field guide, *The Mushroom Handbook,* caught my eye. Louis Krieger, the author, described the symptoms of poisoning by some black-spored mushrooms:

Panaeolus species (now Psilocybe) look harmless enough but it is well to keep them out of the cooking utensils for though it is not violently poisonous, they can be the cause of considerable, momentary anxiety. The effects of the poison become evident almost instantaneously. The symptoms are not unlike those of alcohol intoxication. Conspicuous are, failures of muscular coordination, difficulty in standing, inability to walk, drowsiness, lack of control of the emotions, bloodshot eyes, dilated pupils, incoherent or inappropriate speech (the afflicted laughing inordinately at his own foolish remarks) and visions of dancing and wobbly furniture, combined with glorious color combination. . . . The symptoms appear shortly after the meal. They are exhilaration, staggering gait and queer disturbance of vision. The patients are soon normal.

Momentarily, I thought that if the symptoms of mushroom poisoning included glorious color visions, exhilaration, and especially laughing at one's own foolish remarks (something I had always wanted to be able to do), what could be bad about it? If myth and misconception had dominated attitudes toward edible mushrooms, perhaps those toward psychoactive ones were similarly tainted. Still, this had nothing to do with me.

It was around this time that I attended the 1978 Snowmass Conference on Toxic and Hallucinogenic Mushrooms. Along with a number of doctors and amateur mushroom hunters, I came to the Rockies to hunt fungi and to learn something of the identification, diagnosis, biochemistry, and treatment of mushroom poisoning. At the conference, one speaker clearly dominated. His name was Andrew Weil, and he had been invited to give a lecture each of the five days on various aspects of hallucinogenic mushroom poisoning. Weil had lived for many years on American Indian reservations and in remote villages of Asia and South America, studying the medical and pharmacological uses of plants by indigenous populations. He brought to Snowmass personal knowledge of various psychoactive plants—peyote, daturea, yagé, coca, chili peppers, and, of course, mushrooms. Weil's Peruvian serapes and his bushy beard set him apart from the other participants, but his unorthodox opinions sent a mild shock wave through the audience. A medical doctor by training, Weil presented himself as a humanist-writer-ethnobotanist who was more interested in people's use of and experience with psychoactive drugs and plants than in using his medical authority to eliminate them.

Altered consciousness, or peak experience, said Weil, is really a natural state and is as necessary to mental and physical health as are dreams (which are also states of altered consciousness). We have all experienced highs—in laughter, sex, sports, or spinning games that we played as children—in which we moved into a buoyant, transcendent state. The altered state is a passage connecting our conscious and unconscious minds. "Sometimes I think of the mind as a huge old mansion with many rooms and closed doors," Weil told the audience. "Behind one of those doors is the crazy room, where paranoia, rage, and total chaos reside. And we're all afraid to open that door." I heard a loud rustle of papers around me as he continued: "Although most of us can't admit it, we can all get into that space. I know I can. And I feel much stronger for knowing that part of myself. After all," he said, ignoring the obvious discomfort around him, "the earth is a symbol of solid firmament, isn't it? But just think what it's sitting on. Total chaos, which gives birth to and underlies all order. In different ways, biofeedback, fasting, meditation, and psychoanalysis break down barriers and open doors of communication between the conscious and the unconscious. Hallucinogens, including psychoactive mushrooms, are just another way to do that."

Mushrooms and other mind-altering plants have been used to alter consciousness for thousands of years. They did not originate in Haight-Ashbury in the 1960s. In India and China, in the villages of Brazil and in the mountains of Peru, opium, peyote, yagé, and coca were all used in ritualized ways to divine the future and achieve different (not necessarily higher) states of being. A hallucinogenic extract isolated from ergot, which is the sclerotium or compact mass of threads in which food is stored, of a parasitic mushroom called *Claviceps purpurea*, Weil said, is reported to have been used in the Eleusinian mysteries of ancient Greece. The Zapotecs, the Mazatecs, and other Indians of Mexico have been using various species of *Psilocybe* in their religious rites and divinatory rituals for 3,500 years. Weil wondered aloud why we should be so distraught about something that has been an integral part of so many cultures in so many parts of the world for so many centuries.

It is only since 1957, Weil observed, that the general public in this country has even known that psychoactive mushrooms exist. That was the year that Gordon Wasson published his celebrated May 1957 *Life* magazine article, "In Search of the Magic Mushroom," describing his discovery and use of *Psilocybe* in the Oaxacan highlands and coining the term "magic mushroom." Partly because of Wasson, and partly because of the growing use of LSD in the 1960s and the popularity of Carlos Castañeda, thousands of young people trooped off to Mexico searching for blue mushrooms in green pastures. But they needn't have gone so far away. Almost a dozen species of *Psilocybe* have since been discovered growing wild in the cow pastures and college campuses of the Pacific Northwest and Gulf Coast states. Today, the domes-

*Psilocybe
semilanceata*

tic cultivation of one of those species, *Psilocybe cubensis*, has become a cottage industry whose sales, Weil predicted, could rival those of the supermarket mushroom, *Agaricus bisporus*.

The rustle of papers grew louder as Weil said, "The difference between a drug and a poison is only a matter of degree. Many toxins are beneficial in small doses, but when you increase the dosage of a drug it can become quite dangerous." No doctor—or anyone else—can deny that. But there are drugs and there are "drugs," and drugs used to heal are not viewed in the same way as "narcotics."

Coffee, tobacco, alcohol, and sugar, Weil urged, are among the most potent psychoactive drugs we have. They are toxic and addictive, yet most people don't even view them as drugs. We use them so habitually that we tolerate their effects and we experience no psychoactive response. But if we used them only occasionally, we would get a high from them. He expressed amusement at the idea of coffee breaks and cocktails during and after drug conferences and told the story of the mother whose son was brought into an emergency room after a terrible car accident. "Thank God it was alcohol and not drugs," she had said. "Western culture," said Weil, "arrived where it is by not looking in the direction of the unconscious. Alcohol is a way to screen it out, to turn down the volume of our mind." To stay out of the crazy room, perhaps.

Psychoactive mushrooms, on the other hand, according to Weil, are among the safest groups of drugs. Their toxins and their potential for addiction and pharmacological danger are minimal. Classed as psychedelics, or hallucinogens, psilocybin and psilocyn belong to a group of chemicals called indols, which stimulate the central and sympathetic nervous systems and cause tingling fingers, disorientation, and perceptual changes in colors, sounds, and images of reality. Although we don't know much more than that, it appears that they interact with the body's own chemicals, releasing some and inhibiting others. "The pharmacological power of hallucinogenic mushrooms is a raw, neutral power," said Weil, "that creates changes in the body's feeling, perception, and level of arousal. How we experience that is not [the result of] the drug, but [the result of] the mind."

Not surprisingly, the temperature of the largely medical audience rose several degrees when Weil suggested that what is often called toxic psychosis is really a panic reaction to unexpected sensations. "When someone takes a mind-altering mushroom without realizing it," Weil suggested, "the result might well produce a kind of panic, and when someone is in unfamiliar surroundings, or goes into the experience already under stress, he or she might also get a bad reaction." Weil did not underestimate the

powerful effects of the mushroom, or its psychological
dangers. But the dangers are not toxic psychosis and do
not require medical treatment.

"For thousands of years," Weil went on, "mushrooms
have been used in rituals, which create a safe environment for a powerful and unpredictable experience. Today, recreational use of mushrooms and other drugs is
often totally unritualized and can lead to dependency and
unpleasant, even intolerable experiences." What Weil
called "set and setting" are essential to safe, responsible
use. He advised doctors that where, when, and with whom
drugs are taken is an important part of preventive therapy.

"There is no safe, responsible use of drugs," a voice
called out. "You're asking us to recommend drug use?
We're doctors, not babysitters." With a sedate, polite snap,
the doctors had closed their briefcases and their minds.

One of the things I love about mushrooms is that they
always seem to involve other, seemingly disparate things.
In this case, the disagreement over toxic and hallucinogenic mushroom poisoning reflected the genteel but on-
going hostility between the guardians of the medical, scientific, and social establishments and those who oppose
them. I came to this conference an innocent mycophile,
eager for information; after five days I found myself in
a seriously altered state. The set and setting were right.
Weil's ideas were not only provocative but sane and sensible; they reduced my fears, released my own private
endorphins, and provided me with a natural high as only
ideas, sex, sports, and meditation are also capable of doing.
I thought about coffee, sugar, alcohol, and love—I had
given up cigarettes long ago. In varying degrees they bring
me great pleasure and great pain, and I can't do without
any of them.

I thought about the spinning game called "statues"

that I played as a child with my friends, dizzily twirling one another around and around until we let go, leaving one to "freeze" in the pose of Frankenstein, say, or Venus de Milo. I thought about my own "crazy room," about how many times I have entered it even without drugs, wondering sometimes if all the crazy rooms in the world had been delivered to my house. I thought about Weil's description of our stable planet spinning dizzily in tht total chaos of space, and I wondered if it was because Linnaeus had found mushrooms so disturbing to his own personal sense of order that he had named their biological order *Chaos*.

My experiences with wild edibles had already taught me that there is as much culture and superstition in the word *poison* as there is medicine and biochemistry. Derived from the Latin *potio*, or "drink," poison has been associated for centuries with the idea of a potion—sleeping or more permanent—administered to an innocent princess or an evil king. For part of the general public, the word *poisonous* applies to any mushroom that doesn't grow on the supermarket shelf (despite the fact that the chemicals and preservatives used on the cultivated *Agaricus* can be far more toxic than most mushrooms growing in the wild). While no sane mushroom hunter would deliberately eat a mushroom known to be poisonous, I had learned that most toxins are not fatal but cause only stomachaches, diarrhea, or cold sweats, and sometimes only to some people. There are trace amounts of deadly toxins in some of the most popular and safest edibles. Toxins are identifiable, tangible molecules of organic matter whose behavior can generally be predicted. They are not magic potions or voodoo curses inflicted on us by powerful, unseen enemies. Knowledge and experience had reduced my fear and promoted responsible behavior, and it was through edibles that I learned to react to the word *poison* with caution rather than renunciation.

Over the years, I have learned to parboil honeys and peel the caps from slippery jacks and that most blue-staining boletes are perfectly safe to eat but that otherwise edible species growing on eucalyptus trees, which are toxic, are best to stay away from. Still, the first time I ate a *Lepiota procera*, the parasol, and later on *Amanita rubescens*, the blusher, my family and I lived for twenty-four hours in mortal terror that I had made a dreadful error. The terror was unfounded, of course, for I knew the mushrooms well enough and had not mistaken them for any others. The parasol and the blusher have since turned out to be two of my favorite edibles, and the understanding that knowledge can conquer fear was a heady one.

When it came to psychoactive mushrooms, however, it was a different story. I had never even seen a magic mushroom, and as far as I knew they grew only in books. Nobody I ever knew had taken one; my friends were too old, my kids too young. But now I was full of doubt. Weil's reasoning had taken away all my reasons (perhaps my reason as well) for abstinence. If thousands of young hallucinogen hunters were willing to enter the world of edibles through the doors of perception, why shouldn't I enter the world of psychedelics through the kitchen door? I was convinced that I was ready to try a psychoactive mushroom.

From the accounts I had heard of others' experiences, I knew something of what to expect. For some, it was a quiet, uninterrupted journey, an act of "seeing" connections, truth, God, or interior filmstrips. A four-hour picture show rolls by the window of the mind's eye, featuring tiny geometric shapes and giant, brilliantly colored cities. Waves shimmer with energy. Whole forests dissolve into the threads and fibers of creation. One enthusiastic supporter of the experience reported seeing "incredible lush flowers that make *Yellow Submarine* look

like a black-and-white newsreel. Purple and green phos-
phorescent moss with striped snakes in hot blues, pinks,
and oranges. Thousands of purple bananas flying through
the sky. Sometimes you stand there"—he smiled, re-
membering—"staring at your own hand for hours, wondering what it is and who it belongs to, just trying to
trick it into doing what you want. Sometimes the roof
just opens up, and there you are, flying through the sky
with all those bananas, just looking down at yourself."

But sometimes there is turbulence, and the voyage is
bumpy. Altered visual and auditory perceptions, intense
feelings, powerful insights, and heightened awareness can
transport the traveler not only to heights of ecstasy, but
also to depths of paranoia, loss of identity, and a profound sense of annihilation. The trip then becomes
blinding instead of enlightening. One person's flying bananas become another's attacking Martians. The fear of
crashing due to engine trouble, as in more mundane and
mechanical means of travel, is less than the fear of a
flight through eternity caused by defective landing gear;
the fear of an interplanetary hijacker is far greater than
that of one from Beirut.

Three weeks after Weil's lecture, while hunting in the
California woods, I met Bill and Dave, two young men
who were scouring the forest for *Amanita muscaria.* Dave
noticed the bright red ones I had collected in my basket.
I told him I could never resist *muscaria.* They were com-
pelling to pick, although I knew I would never eat them.
Could he have them? Of course! Would I show him where
there were others? Dave looked at me directly. There
was no subterfuge in his eyes or in his voice. Mushrooms create camaraderie.

I didn't blink when Bill told me why they wanted the
muscaria: to connect with mankind's ancient past in order to warn others about the future. He was a tall stringy

figure with long blond hair and self-consciously beatific eyes. He reminded me of someone. Jesus, perhaps. He looked like the type of person that always speaks in metaphors. I told Bill and Dave that from what I had heard, *muscaria* isn't as good as its reputation would have it; it is suspiciously toxic, and the side effects of nausea and vomiting don't seem worth the slight change in consciousness. While we were on the subject, I boldly asked if they knew anything about *Psilocybe* or magic mushrooms.

Bill reached into a pocket of his torn overalls and pulled out a razor blade, some dirty Kleenex, two balloons, and a plastic bag, which he spread out on the ground. He reached in and pulled out about a dozen mushrooms, shriveled and dried beyond recognition, that could have been *Conocybes, Inocybes, Coprini, Psathyrellae,* or any of a dozen other kinds of LBMs, mostly inedible, some mildly to seriously toxic, and one, a *Galerina,* deadly poisonous. Sensible mushroom hunters keep all of them away from the table. At least the *muscaria* looks magical. Carefully, Dave went over them one by one. They were all species of *Psilocybe: baeocystis, cyanescens, stuntzii;* the larger ones were *cubensis.* Bill grew these himself; they didn't grow wild around here, and they were easy to cultivate. Did I want to try them?

Well . . . I hesitated. Yes, but I wanted to know some things first. How did he know what they were? What were the identifying characters? How much should I take? Where would I do it? What would happen? How should I eat them? Dave answered my questions patiently, but Bill interrupted: "Trust and fear!" he said. "That is all there is to it. The mushroom only speaks to you if you trust it." I clearly didn't. "It will not work if you are afraid." And I clearly was, he added. The Indians, he said, had confronted their fear by eating the mushrooms with eggs. I admitted that I was afraid, which was precisely why I was asking all these questions. "Don't look away," he commanded. "Trust me."

Under the circumstances, that wasn't easy. Bill told me that I was allowing my intellect to control me. My soul would never soar as long as it was bound to my mind. The mind is a prison. The sky is a prism through which the soul divides and multiplies its energies. He talked of white lights and crystals, pulling from his pocket a small diamond-shaped glass, which he warmed in his hand, telling me it contained the entire universe. I could not see it, however, as long as I was afraid. With proper guidance, I could learn to trust. I would then be able to project and travel to any planet, star, or supernova in this galaxy and beyond. My soul would leave my body on earth, and once free it would expand until it was the universe itself. Bill's voice remained monochromatic, slow and gentle, but his eyes darkened imperceptibly with each leg of the journey. Slowly, I began to realize that he wasn't speaking in metaphors.

I knew I was in California, but this was more than I had bargained for. I wasn't even sure that a twenty-minute bus ride with Bill would be bearable, never mind an eternity together in outer space. I looked at Dave for help. He saw the plea in my eyes and began to talk. "Let's be practical about this," he said. "The world is in for difficult times—pollution, war, poverty. They're all going to get worse. The world may even blow itself up." I nodded in agreement. "Well, then," he continued, "we're all going to need to find someplace else to go, aren't we? And only those of us"—Dave paused, allowing his reasonable words to penetrate—"who have the tools to get there are going to be saved." But the sinking ship, planet earth, still looked safer to me than Bill and Dave's lifeboat. I politely refused their offer of mushrooms and salvation. I was not yet ready.

Within a three-month period in the following fall, I heard several stories about people I knew or knew about who, after what they had believed to be a perfectly standard mushroom meal, had found themselves distinctly weak in the knees and limbs, victims of uncontrollable fits of laughter, sometimes embarrassing themselves and others at public meetings. Laughing at their own foolish remarks, perhaps.

Stories of accidental ingestion of hallucinogenic mushrooms are, of course, nothing new. The literature is full of cases of such—reports of mushroom hunters searching for edibles, picking *Psilocybe* by mistake, and reacting with bouts of silliness, intoxication, and sometimes panic. But hallucinogenic mushroom "poisoning," whether accidental or intentional, had been a phenomenon occurring primarily in the West Coast and Gulf states, the two areas where they grow wild most prolifically. These latest cases were all in the Northeast. They involved reasonably experienced mycophages who were not prone to mushroom adventures, and all had taken place within a three-month period. All three misidentifications involved the honey mushroom, one of our most popular and plentiful edibles. Was this mushroom developing new properties? Was there a new mushroom in the area that so closely resembled the honey that it was difficult to tell them apart? (Honeys have frequently been confused with the poisonous jack o'lantern and once that I know of with the deadly *Galerina,* but never as far as I knew with any laughter-causing species.) I was intrigued.

The guilty mushroom turned out to be the one called *Gymnopilus spectabilis,* which, like the honey, is a yellowish-to-orangy-brown mushroom with a ring, growing in autumn in large clusters on trees, stumps, and buried wood. Unlike the honey or the jack o'lantern, it has a rusty rather than a white spore print (although experienced mushroom hunters often neglect to take one).

Gymnopilus spectabilis

Although *Gymnopilus spectabilis* slightly resembles the honey in appearance, it is difficult to understand how anyone, upon tasting it, could confuse the two. Whatever laughter and pleasure are caused by the former, they are not the result of the eating itself: the mushroom is extremely bitter, sometimes unpalatable.

Although *Gymnopilus spectabilis* is taxonomically unrelated to the magic mushrooms, psilocybin and psilocyn have been discovered in some collections of it that were tested at the University of Michigan. In Japan, it is called "big laughing mushroom." *Gymnopilus spectabilis* has appeared on occasion at forays, although in most older field guides it is tucked away among the innocuous inedibles. The mushroom seemed to be common enough, but I don't remember ever seeing it in the woods and probably wouldn't know it if I fell over it.

A few weeks later, as I was coming home from my morning run, passing the entrance to Central Park not three blocks from my home, I saw a cluster of small orange mushrooms poking out from under some weeds. I picked them and walked home, mentally leafing through all the possibilities. None seemed right.

The gills were an orangy brown; so was the spore print. The field guides were of little help. I called a friend who knew more about mushrooms than I did. He looked at the spore print, looked at the mushroom, looked at some spores under the microscope, and looked at me. "What is it?" he asked, smiling. I shook my head. "What does it look like?" he prodded, as he always does, never coming right out and saying what he thinks. "Honey, jack o'lantern, *Pholiota*—" Then I stopped. "*Gymnopilus spectabilis?*" He nodded that it was. "Let's eat it," I said, much to my own surprise. Here was a serious and curious mycophile like me, who knew his identification and had eaten magic mushrooms and had returned to earth unharmed. If he would, then I would; if he wouldn't, then I wouldn't. "Sure," he said, "but I don't think there's enough here for a mouse to get high on." "Well, then," I said, "let's find some more."

I scoured the woods in New Jersey and Westchester. Nothing. "My woods are full of them," said a friend in Connecticut. But that was the week before I got there.

A few days later, poking among those same weeds in Central Park, I uncovered another small cluster of the same mushroom. I could hardly contain myself. "Barely enough for a pigeon," my friend said. (The hallucinogenic properties in *Gymnopilus* are weaker than those in *Psilocybe* and require a much larger dose.) "We'll wait," I said. "Let them grow. It can't take more than a few weeks." "In New York City? Are you crazy?" If it had been anything else, I would have agreed. Only mushrooms, I thought, could last in Central Park for more than fifteen minutes without being kicked, stolen, or written on. And I was right. I checked them daily, and within a week they were the size of tiny persimmons. "You don't have to look every day," my friend warned. "New Yorkers are curious. They see you crawling around there every day, and they want to know what's going on." I looked around at the old people sitting on benches and at the children on tricycles and skateboards, at students from a nearby school hanging out during lunch. People in this city spend thousands of dollars on drugs, I thought, and here are pounds of a glorious hallucinogen growing right under their noses. The greatest danger, I decided, was from the neighborhood dogs who sniffed, roamed about, and marked their territory in the immediate area. I told my friend *he* was paranoid.

The mushrooms continued to grow and I to inspect them, picking the largest to make room for the others. I already had five large fruiting bodies that weighed eight ounces each. There must have been two to three pounds there, enough for two people. The mushrooms were growing through the weeds, visible to any curious child or passerby. "They're big enough," said my friend; "let's not be greedy." But success for me was becoming itself like a drug that triggered off the need for more success, and I wanted to wait until they were as large as grapefruits. I would wake up each morning anxious to know if they were still there, if they had grown even larger. "Let's wait for a full moon," I suggested. Someone had told me that a full moon passes its energy to mushrooms, geometrically intensifying their power. "Okay," he said, "but don't say I didn't warn you if they're eaten first by werewolves."

The night sky was cloudless and the moon looked to be a perfect circle, but I had checked the newspaper just to make sure. It was a warm October evening; one of New York's nighttime subcultures gathered only yards away. "This is the most ridiculous thing I've ever seen," he said. "This is probably the busiest corner in the city—you might just as well put up a stand and charge five cents." He stood impatiently with his hands in his pockets as, ignoring him, I hurried my task and carefully removed the mushrooms, placing them in a large Bloomingdale's shopping bag. A mushroom basket would, I admitted, have looked a little conspicuous at that time of night. Moreover, the mushrooms needed to be shielded from the eyes of passersby in order to retain their power—and I was especially concerned about the patrol car lurking outside the park entrance. (The police had frequently stopped me as I carried armfuls of mushrooms through the city streets—mostly, however, out of solicitous concern that they might be poisonous.)

At my house, we spread the mushrooms out on the table. "Remember," my friend warned, "we don't even know if these are psychoactive." I knew only that some samples tested in Michigan had proved to contain psilocybin. Out west, where magic mushrooms grow like weeds, *Gymnopilus* is a complete dud. And I only knew a handful of Easterners who had eaten them, intentionally or otherwise. I particularly loved the idea that we might have an experience that is not possible in California. "Of course they're psychoactive," I said, separating out the largest, most golden specimens. "How many do we need?" "That many," he answered as he took a clump and weighed them until the scale read eight ounces. "That's a lot of mushrooms to eat," I said. "I hope they taste good." I took a nibble and grimaced. "I'll never get it down." He suggested, "Maybe we should wait until the morning and get some painkillers." "No!" I insisted, and began to scour the cupboards and refrigerator for culinary taste inhibitors. "Maybe they won't taste as bad sautéed with lots of butter." They did. An omelette? I remembered what Bill and Dave had told me about Indians, fear, and eggs; in this case, the conquest of taste took priority. Onions, of course. Then we added apples, walnuts, powdered sugar, and all the combinations we could think of that would possibly blot out the taste of the mushrooms. They didn't. "Maybe this is not meant to be," I said. "Maybe this is why these mushrooms will never catch on," he said.

The shutters are drawn and the room is dark. In the distance a voice is chanting strange nasal sounds that perhaps are human but are of no recognizable language. It is the voice of Maria Sabina, Mazatec shaman, coming not from an adobe hut on the other side of North America but from two speakers across the room. She is invoking the mushroom to speak. "In the name of Jesus," I can barely make out. In the name of wisdom and truth, I suspect. From my unconscious I bring forth four Indian warriors climbing the tiny stone steps of a temple. They are almost naked, decked out only in feathered headdress and jaguar mask. At the top, the high priest awaits, to award them a prize, to pluck the moon from the sky, to pluck out their hearts. I cannot keep my eyes from their naked loins. . . .

My friend stands up from the sofa and goes to the record player, his gait unsteady. The chanting stops. "This is ridiculous," he says. "We're not in Mexico and Maria Sabina isn't holding her evening vigil. We're in New York City and this is an Upper West Side mushroom, growing in our own backyard, right in front of old people, dogs, and city kids. That's where its power comes from." He places another record on the turntable, and from the darkness another very human voice belts out, "Love that's fresh and still unspoiled. Love that's only slightly soiled . . ." It's the voice of Ella Fitzgerald. "And that's our New York Maria Sabina," my friend whispers contentedly.

"What if we made a mistake?" I sit up with some difficulty. He looks at his watch. "We'd know by now. Jack o'lantern poison takes only thirty minutes, and more than an hour has gone by."

"What if it's an *Amanita*?"

"You don't feel that for twelve hours. And they don't have orange spores. They don't even look anything like these. Besides, why has the poor *Amanita* become the symbol of guilt for all mushroom hunters?"

"But we didn't take a spore print. Oh, my God, we should have. Maybe there were two kinds of mushrooms growing in the same spot and one was a new kind of deadly species. Unseen by the human eye." I begin to laugh. "What if they are honeys? They'll take us to the emergency room, write us up in the medical journals: 'Toxic psychosis from accidental ingestion of edible mushrooms.' "

"They didn't taste very edible," he says.

"What if we ate the right mushroom, but we just didn't eat enough?"

He smiles. "Then we'll probably just get smaller and smaller."

I get up to open the shutters. Released from bondage, the moon crashes through the windowpane, splinters into a thousand pieces, and darts around the room bouncing off walls. For a very long time, we lie quietly on the sofa, looking up at a display of changing colors. It is hard to talk; to move would be impossible. Out of nowhere, I begin to laugh, a tiny giggle at first. "What's so funny?"

he asks. "The colors," I say. "They're so blah. Why are we wasting our time looking at them?" "That's not funny," he says.

We are quiet for another very long time, until he begins to laugh. For the next three hours nothing and everything is funny. My mother calls to wish me happy birthday. She wants to know what is wrong. Why am I laughing so much? "Why is laughing wrong?" I ask her. It is a strange feeling, laughter connected to nothing—and to everything. It begins to hurt, but I can't stop, and suddenly I begin to understand that my laughter is a purely physical response having nothing to do with anything being funny. It is a natural high triggered by a drug. That would normally make me cry, but now it only makes me laugh harder.

He sits up and falls back again, finally lifting himself and staggering toward the door. "It's hard," he says. I follow him out the front door and across the street into the park, barely able to walk. "What's hard?" "Walking." His voice has the singsong appeal of a very young child's. I assure him that if he tries really hard, he can do it. It is just a question of putting one foot in front of the other. He struggles bravely, but it isn't so easy. Then, what seems like hours later, he stands upright and smiles proudly. "I can do it. I can do it," he calls, and starts waltzing, then running through the park, waving his hand mysteriously in the air. "Say good-bye to the monkeys," he instructs me, "I'm walking upright."

It was like watching the achievement of bipedalism replayed—the birth of a brand-new species. "You did it," I say, taking his hand and walking with him across the savannah of Central Park, waving good-bye to the monkeys.

CHAPTER 11

Curiouser and Curiouser

In a few minutes the caterpillar took the hookah out of its mouth, and got down off the mushroom, and crawled away into the grass, merely remarking as it went "the top will make you grow taller, and the stalk will make you grow shorter."

"The top of what? The stalk of what?" thought Alice.

"Of the mushroom," said the caterpillar, just as if she had asked it aloud and in another moment was out of sight.

—LEWIS CARROLL,
Alice's Adventures in Wonderland

ALICE'S ADVENTURES UN-DERGROUND certainly included a disconcertingly large number of extreme size changes. First she followed the instructions on the bottle labeled DRINK ME, then she proceeded to the cake marked EAT ME, continued to an unlabeled bottle, and finally to the mushroom upon which the caterpillar sat. After drinking from the bottle, Alice shrank to so small a size that her chin struck her foot; then her neck grew so long that she could see neither her shoulders nor her hands, and she was accused by a pigeon of being a serpent. After several nibbles of the mushroom, alternating cap and stalk, Alice grew "sometimes taller and sometimes shorter, until she had succeeded in bringing herself down to her usual size."

For over a century, scholars and psychoanalysts have been interpreting Alice's adventures as a dream vision, as a journey into the underground of the unconscious filled with symbols, as an Oedipal fixation, as time distortions, and as a metaphysical puzzle. Yet few refer to Alice's frequent episodes of macropsia, in which the perceptual distortions of size and distance that take place lead her to bang her head against a ceiling, to put her arm through a chimney, and to all but drown in a pool of her own tears. Surely such experiences must have been as unsettling for Alice and worthy of the same scholarly attention as her exposure to the frenzied world inhabited by a mad hatter, a nervous rabbit, and a megalomaniacal queen. And I could find no references in the *Annotated Alice: Alice's Adventures in Wonderland and Through the Looking Glass,* edited with notes by Martin Gardner, to what the bottles or the cake might have contained or to the caterpillar's hookah and his seemingly drugged behavior. As for the mushroom he sat upon, Gardner makes one reference to nameless old books about certain kinds of hallucinogenic mushrooms that Lewis Carroll may have read. What is the mushroom? What are the old books? *Alice's Adventures in Wonderland* was as integral a part of my and my children's childhoods as lost mittens and notes from the teacher were, but it was only after I began to read books about mushrooms that I made a con-

nection between Lewis Carroll's imagination and historical fact. During the eighteenth and nineteenth centuries, soldiers and traders returned to Europe from Siberia with eyewitness accounts of strange practices among Siberian tribespeople. The earliest known report is the journal entry of a Polish prisoner of war in 1658 describing the habits of the Ob-Ugrian Ostyak in Western Siberia. In his search for the cultural and etymological roots of mushrooms, Gordon Wasson uncovered many of these old stories and reported them in his book *Soma, the Divine Mushroom of Immortality*. He describes how the Siberians "eat certain fungi in the shape of fly agarics, and thus get drunk worse than on vodka." A Swedish colonel who spent twelve years in a Siberian prison describes the practices of the Koryakt tribe in the Northeast.

> The Russians who trade with them carry thither a Kind of Mushrooms, called in the Russian Tongue, Muchumor, which they exchange for Squirils, Fox, Hermin, Sable, and other Furs: Those who are rich among them, lay up large Provisions of these Mushrooms, for the Winter. When they make a Feast, they pour Water upon some of these Mushrooms, and boil them. Then they drink the Liquor, which intoxicates them.

The mushroom described is the *Amanita muscaria*, known around the world as fly agaric: *Fliegenpilz* or *Fliegenschwamm* (German for "fly mushroom"); *fausse-orange* or *tue-mouche* (French for "false Caesar's mushroom" and "fly killer"); and *mukhomor* (Russian for "fly killer"). Used for centuries as an insecticide, the mushroom's ability to kill flies appears to be more mythical than real (although it has been known to kill cats).

In the literature of many cultures, the fly itself is associated with madness or divine possession. In the New Testament (Matt. 12:24) Beelzebub, the Lord of the Flies, is portrayed as the prince of demons. In *Faust*, Goethe refers to the "Fly-God, Destroyer, Liar." In Nordic mythology, the god Loki assumes the appearance of a fly in order to enter the chambers of sleeping goddesses. Hieronymus Bosch illustrated flies in their demonic role. And in the Middle Ages, delirium, drunkenness, and insanity were attributed to insects loose inside the victim's head. Today, we talk of a bee in the bonnet, a bug in the ear, or bats in the belfry.

In the light of the Siberian reports of the mushroom's effects, its linguistic association to the fly of madness does not appear to be an accident. After ingestion, muscles would shake and jerk, often followed by dizziness or vomiting and then by a long vision-filled sleep, sometimes inhabited by mythical beasts; sometimes the inebriant would find himself in a magical flower garden surrounded by beautiful women dressed in white. After rousing from these visions, the intoxicant might experience an unusual sense of well-being and extravagant heights of gaiety in which he would jump around, dance, and sing. Sometimes he would find himself seized with sudden bursts of extraordinary energy. After twelve to sixteen hours, another sleep would follow, this one uninterrupted and peaceful, after which the participant would awake, perhaps a little low in spirit, but without the headaches and other symptoms associated with alcohol.

Three different Siberian accounts are sprinkled liberally with references to macropsia, the disorder that was experienced so intensely by Alice.

> Some might deem a small crack to be as wide as a door, and a tub of water as deep as the sea [Or perhaps a pool of tears?].

All things appear to him increased in size. For instance, when entering a room and stepping over the door-sill, he will raise his feet exceedingly high. The handle of a knife seems to him so big that he wants to grasp it with both hands.

The senses become deranged; surrounding objects appear either very large or very small.

Although we cannot be certain that Lewis Carroll read these Siberian reports, many of them were translated into English and circulated in England and the United States. We know that Oliver Goldsmith paraphrased one account in *The Citizen of the World,* published in 1721. The scarlet-and-white-spotted *Amanita muscaria* illustrated in *Alice's Adventures in Wonderland* is a common mushroom in the English woodlands, and Alice's symptoms correspond so closely to the reports of the Siberian travelers that it is likely that Lewis Carroll at least knew of them and of their hallucinogenic properties.

In the 1940s, Gordon Wasson read the same accounts from Siberia. Since there are so few references to the fly agaric that are not influenced in some way by Gordon Wasson, it is difficult to imagine the mushroom without the man or to know whether he singlehandedly elevated the fly agaric to an archetypal experience or actually uncovered an authentic ancient cult that had lain for centuries enveloped in mystery.

Wasson's involvement with mushrooms began in 1927, on his honeymoon in New York's Catskill Mountains, when his Russian-born wife Valentina saw some and suddenly darted from his side to gather them. Her soft endearments and cries of ecstasy were matched only by his own fear of the "poisonous," "putrid," and "disgusting" toadstools. She cooked and served some that night; others she dried for winter use. Wasson refused to eat a single one. Few modern marriages would survive so profound and irreconcilable a difference; for the Wassons, it was merely the first step in a thirty-year journey of two minds devoted to unearthing the roots of that difference.

Digging among the ruins of ancient languages and folklore, the Wassons emerged with what he called a "bold and some would say wild surmise" that more than six thousand years ago our ancestors had worshipped a divine mushroom. Further research and their reading of the Siberian accounts convinced the Wassons that the mushroom was the fly agaric and that current mycophobia had its roots in the fear and awe inspired by an early powerful religious experience. "As man groped his way out from his lowly past," wrote Wasson, "the mushrooms revealed to him worlds on a different plane of being, a heaven and perhaps a hell. For the credulous primitive mind, the mushrooms must have reinforced mightily the idea of the miraculous and one is emboldened to the point of asking whether they may not have planted in primitive man the very idea of God."

Having established a link between the "fly" in the German word *Fliegenpilz* ("fly mushroom") and the idea of divine madness, Wasson went on to seek the roots of the aversion to toads and toadstools in Anglo-Saxon culture, an attitude that is at odds with those "divine" associations, and unlike the feelings of previous cultures. "In the pagan pantheon," he says, "the toad occupied an honored place." The mushroom's first link with treachery and lechery came in the early Christian era, when reverence turned to revulsion. Why, Wasson asks, is there no Anglo-Saxon word for the *Amanita muscaria*? And why, at the same time, is the fear-filled word *toadstool* a generalized term that refers to all poisonous mushrooms and to none in particular? Because, he concludes, the toadstool and the *A. muscaria* are one and the same. Wasson draws his clues from China, from the Basque country, and from regions of France, where *ha-ma-chun*, *amoroto*, and *crapaudin*, respectively, refer specifically to the fly agaric; all mean "toad mushroom" or "toad-like thing."

From there it was only a hop, skip, and a jump for Wasson to the long-sought-after identity of the plant juice drunk by Soma, the plant god of ancient India first immortalized in the Rig Veda; his flowing juices transported Hindu priests to flights of religious ecstasy. The botanical identity of Soma (which is the name of both the drink and the god) has remained a mystery for over two thousand years and has been a major focus of English Vedic scholarship ever since the eighteenth century, when the Sanskrit Vedas were first translated into English.

Any number of plants had been suggested and rejected as the source of Soma's inspiration: climbing shrubs, creepers, rhubarb, fermented liquor, *Cannabis sativa*. But none of them had all the qualities of the Soma drink that were contained in the rapturous verses of the Vedic hymns. Soma is compared to the sun, both when red and when gold, and to Agni, the Hindu god of fire who grows on mountaintops. The Soma plant is said to lack roots, leaves, and blossoms. For Wasson, the evidence pointed directly to the fly agaric: its red and yellow variations; its preferred association with birch, which in India grows only in the mountains near the Indus valley; its rootless, seedless, and leafless character; and the milky yellow juice and its powerful impact that was described over and over again by the soldiers and travelers among the tribesmen of Siberia.

Over the centuries, the identity of the original plant was lost. Later generations replaced it with substitutes that were similar to the original in one character or another, but none of them possessed all of its qualities. To Wasson, as we will see, this substitution was another point of evidence linking *muscaria* to the original Soma.

When the Aryans invaded the Indus Valley, Wasson argues, they brought with them from the north the Vedic language and a sacred mushroom cult that was well integrated into their agricultural-warrior society. Moreover, *A. muscaria* forms a mutually beneficial, or mycorrhizal, relationship with the roots of birch trees, and birch was the tree most commonly associated with Siberian shamanism. Buriat tribesmen bow both morning and night to the birches planted in front of their huts, and during his rites of ecstasy the shaman climbs a birch as a symbolic ascent to heaven. Siberian mythology is filled with references to the birch as the tree of life. In one myth, a middle-aged woman, representing the birch spirit, emerges naked to her waist out of the roots of the tree. From her swollen breast she offers milk to a youthful devotee, whose strength thereupon immediately increases by a hundred times.

In northern Eurasia, birch grows only at sea level. In the Indus Valley, it is found only at heights of between eight and sixteen thousand feet. Before the Aryans left their northern homeland, where the mushroom was plentiful, the fly agaric had to be dried; it was transported over the long distance and was used sparingly. The Aryans conquered only the valleys, and their source in the mountains for fly agaric remained in enemy hands. Over the centuries, says Wasson, although Soma's sacred ceremony remained intact, the unavailability of the mushroom forced so many substitutions that it lost its original identity.

Another of Wasson's clues is the frequent reference to two forms of consuming Soma. In the first it is taken directly by eating the mushroom raw or drinking its juice, either plain or mixed with water, milk and curds, honey or herbs. The second form is expressed in the verse that reads, "The swollen men piss the flowing [Soma]." Most Vedic scholars believed *piss* to be a metaphor for water, rain, or earthly nourishment. Wasson believed otherwise—that it was not a metaphor at all. In the Siberian accounts there are many references to the drinking of urine as a way of ingesting the mushroom's power. Among the Koryak tribes, according to one account, *mukhomor* (Russian for fly agaric) is so highly valued that those who have taken it are not permitted to urinate on the ground. They are provided with a dish from which those who cannot afford the price of the mushroom drink the urine and thereby become intoxicated, too. In some cases, the mushroom's power is reported to be so great that it lasts through four or five people.

It is also reported that reindeer in the region have a special passion for both human urine and the fly agaric. In the presence of either, these semi-domesticated animals become quite unmanageable.

Wasson adduces several poetic metaphors that run through the Soma hymns: the "mainstay of the heavens," the "udder," and the "navel." Wasson relates Soma, as the navel of the earth, the navel of heaven, to the womb and childbirth, and he traces the metaphor through the fungal vocabularies of other cultures. In Russia, *pup* means "navel" and *pupyry* means "fungal growth." In contemporary Cambodia, *pzat* means both "navel" and "mushroom." In Turkey, Wasson discovered, *gobek mantari* ("shaggy mane") refers to the navel mushroom. Today's English-language mycological terminology includes the words *umbilical* and *umbonate*, which mean "navel" or "nipple-shaped," and the genus *Omphalia* derives its name from the Greek word for "navel."

Wasson's scholarship and his skill in weaving arguments can hardly be ignored. His conclusions regarding Soma are another matter, better left to those Vedic

scholars who may or may not want their mysteries unraveled by an outsider, or who may not want their mysteries unraveled at all, or who simply find his arguments
weak and his evidence specious.

As for the role of the fly agaric as man's earliest object
of religious devotion, I am far more intrigued by Wasson's relentless obsession than by whether it was or
wasn't. Wasson, the son of a Montana minister, found
his own religion in an hallucinogenic mushroom worshipped thousands of years ago. He found the mushroom
at the core of every activity he explored and saw the
mushroom in every nook and cranny of mythology,
metaphor, and history. (Curiously, he seems to have
overlooked a story known to every child in the Christian
world. Could the red-capped resident of the far north
who flies through the heavens driving reindeer be anything but a fly-agaric-inspired metaphor?)

To John Allegro, a biblical scholar noted for his trans-
lations of the Dead Sea Scrolls, *Amanita muscaria* is no
metaphor at all. The whole Judeo-Christian tradition, he
argues, has its roots in a much older fertility cult that
centered on the fly agaric, and Christ was merely a personification of that cult—a metaphor for the mushroom.
In his book *The Sacred Mushroom and the Cross*, Allegro traces the secret names of mushrooms back to Sumerian tablets and to both the Old and the New Testa-
ments, asserting that the historical accuracy of biblical
events is irrelevant. The "word" is all.

Esau, says Allegro, comes from the Sumerian *e-sh-u-
a*, which means "raised canopy" (or cap), and Esau's
brother's name, Jacob, or *ia-a-gub*, refers to the "pillar"
(or stem). Jacob, according to Allegro, is therefore the
stem of the fungus, and his "red-skinned" brother Esau
is the scarlet cap of the fly agaric.

In the Garden of Eden the serpent and mushroom become one. "Both emerged from holes in the ground," writes Allegro, "in a manner reminiscent of the erection of the sexually aroused penis." The stalk of the mushroom arises from its volva, or "covered basket," as Moses, "the emergent serpent," was born in his papyrus ark, and Jesus in his "manger" or "covered basket." The death and resurrection of Jesus parallels the events of the fertility myth. Born of a miracle, Jesus dies and returns to life. Allegro relates his death and resurrection to being raised up like the serpent of Moses: "As Moses lifted up the serpent in the wilderness so shall the son of man be lifted up, so that all who believe in him have everlasting life" (John 3:14).

As Wasson and Allegro interpret history, one is tempted to interpret *them*. What are they looking for? In fixing on the mushroom as the navel of all spiritual origins, are they very different from poets and philosophers who fix on love, class struggle, or the collective unconscious as the single force behind all human experience?

I didn't realize how close they may have come to something profound until one day I was reading Freud's *Interpretation of Dreams* and came upon the following passage.

> Even in the best interpreted dreams, there is often a place that must be left in the dark, because in the process of interpreting one notices a tangle of dream-thoughts arising which resists unravelling but has also made no further contributions to the dream content.
>
> This then is the navel of the dream, the place where it straddles the unknown. The dream-thoughts, to which interpretation leads one, are necessarily interminable and branch out on all sides into the netlike entanglement of our world of thought. Out of one of the denser places in this meshwork, the dream-wish rises like a mushroom out of its mycelium.

Even for Freud, debunker of myth and relentless seeker of truth, there are certain things that are better left unexplored.

What of the *Amanita muscaria* and its worshippers today? The mushroom itself is alive and well, a common weed, in spring, summer, and fall, depending on the region of the country and whether there is birch, pine, or Douglas fir growing in the area. As for its followers, the *Amanita muscaria* is probably the most-painted and most-photographed of all mushrooms. There isn't an amateur mycologists' photo contest or slide show that doesn't contain at least one fly agaric entry. Gift shops from coast to coast feature dishtowels, needlepoint, and ceramic *chotchkes* with this red-capped beauty (pale to golden yellow in the eastern United States) in all its stages, from tiny button to flaring parasol.

As an edible, *A. muscaria* is shunned by these devout photographers and by most other mushroom hunters. For years, it was described in field guides as deadly, not so surely deadly as *Amanita virosa* or *phalloides*, but deadly in the sense of resembling a drive down a mountain road in Mexico. The mushroom *could* be fatal, experts warned, if you ate too many. What's too many? It depends on the individual. It depends on the collection. It depends on the color of the cap. It depends on the region. But fatalities from *muscaria* have never been proven, and most authorities now admit that the mushroom is not deadly. It is toxic, however, and can cause loss of muscle coordination, dizziness, and severe vomiting.

There are those who eat it. In Italy and Japan, people have been eating it for years as food, ignoring the admonitions, uninterested in its religious power. After boiling the mushroom, they throw away the water and suffer neither ill effects nor altered states. Most of them have never even heard of Gordon Wasson.

As we know from peyote, *Psilocybe,* and other plant hallucinogens, one generation's ritual is another's recreation, and one century's heavenly ascent is another's astral projection. Among drug users, enthusiasm for the mushroom continues unabated in the woods of southern California and in the pages of *High Times* and *Psychedelic Review.*

I was very curious, but only a little tempted, to try it myself. But before I would even consider the possibility, I wanted to find out all I could from living beings whose bodies and souls had survived the experience. It seems that at every mushroom foray there is at least one young drug enthusiast who saunters into the conference hoping to make a connection, often finding himself or herself later converted to "straight" edibles. Since 1976, there have been almost yearly conferences devoted to the cultivation and understanding of hallucinogens. And there were also my own children and their friends and classmates, who have now come of age, and the street people on their California campus. I borrowed their copies of *High Times* and talked to them all. When they heard I was "into" mushrooms, there was no uncomfortable small talk, no shortage of conversation. Almost all of them have eaten, if not cultivated, magic mushrooms, but far fewer knew *muscaria,* and the testimony of those who did was curiously contradictory and hardly more enlightening than the old warnings of mycophobic mycologists.

They report eating from one to several caps. They have eaten the mushroom raw, dried, and cooked. They have thrown away the peel and eaten the mushroom, and they have thrown away the mushroom and eaten the peel. Some claim that only the red variety is potent; others swear by the eastern yellow variety. Few have had the same experience twice, and few seem to have the same experience as others. Sometimes there is no reaction at all. Sometimes there is only nausea and vomiting. Others describe long vision-filled sleep alternating with bursts of amazing energy—all in language curiously similar to the most colorful accounts from Siberia. On a trip to Oregon several years ago, I was given a package of four carefully picked, carefully dried scarlet caps. These were just right, my donor assured me, as long as I didn't eat for twelve hours and only then took them with milk. Would I grow taller or shorter? I wanted to know.

Tom Robbins, West Coast author and mushroom hunter, wrote in a 1976 article for *High Times*, "I have eaten the fly agaric three times. On the second of those occasions I experienced nothing but a slight nausea. The other times I got gloriously, colossally drunk." Gordon Wasson, who tried the mushroom twice, had disappointing results. "We ate them raw, on empty stomachs. We drank the juice on empty stomachs. We mixed the juice with milk and drank the mixture, always on empty stomachs. We felt nauseated and some of us threw up. We fell into a deep slumber from which shouts could not rouse us. . . . In this state I once had vivid dreams, but nothing like what happened when I took *Psilocybe* mushrooms in Mexico, where I did not sleep at all."

Wasson has argued that the Soma-Siberian variant is the only really potent one. Andrew Weil believes that *muscaria* is a "second-rate" hallucinogen. "It was all they had in Siberia," he told me. "You can't imagine how cold those Siberian winters are, but as soon as the Russians introduced vodka, it replaced *muscaria*." Others have suggested that the Siberian tribespeople must have added some other substance to the fly agaric to increase its potency.

The students and bio-assays of chemists have been somewhat more revealing. The two major active components in *muscaria* are ibotenic acid and muscimol, which were isolated in the 1960s and found to be the components responsible for the delirium, the trancelike sleep, the macropsia, and the nausea and dizziness implicated in *muscaria* intoxication. Recent tests have shown that the yellow and orange varieties are equally as potent (or impotent) as the scarlet; this information is confirmed by several of my informants. Bio-assays have also shown that the mushroom varies chemically from individual to individual, collection to collection, and region to region. Michael Beug, professor of chemistry at Evergreen State College in Washington, cautions that the dosage-response ratio is very close. "You can take a certain dose and nothing happens," he says. "Then a bite more, and *pow!*"

What is going on here? What accounts for the difference between these lukewarm, contradictory descriptions and the rapturous accounts of the Siberian travelers? Is it simply that the power of suggestion is greater than the power of the mushroom itself? Or is our current failure to experience the mushroom's effects simply due to our refusal to believe in it? Ultimately, I'm not sure the answer really matters. Any mushroom that can drive eight reindeer across the sky and provide Alice with some of her greatest adventures in Wonderland has demonstrated its power without pharmacological or etymological validation. That's proof enough for me.

CHAPTER 12

The Last Foray

Ɪɴ ᴛʜᴇ Eᴀsᴛ, ꜰᴀʟʟ'ꜱ footsteps are growing faint. The motley colors of autumn leaves fade, and frost brushes against the earth. Mushroom hunters are reduced to foraging for dregs—the ragged *Russulae* and commonplace *Collybia dryophila*. But until the earth is buried under snow, until the trees have broken under the weight of the next glaciation, we grub among the brambles and climb the highest branches. We gladly eat sand for a taste of *Laccaria trullisata*, which grows in the dunes at the edge of the world. Then we dig in the snow for winter mushrooms and cut holes in the ice and fish for oyster mushrooms. Until the last tree is logged, we haunt our old hunting grounds.

It is Halloween night, and while normal people are stringing toilet paper from trees and putting raw eggs in their neighbors' mailboxes, mushroom hunters are out in the woods, our paths illuminated by glowworms and fireflies, by jack o'lanterns decorating old stumps and logs, and by the eerie blue-green light of the *Armillariella mellea*. Two weeks ago, I would have been happy never to see another honey mushroom. Today I know that when they go, it is all over. Each November, as the sun drops behind the winter clouds, I feel as though it is the last season of all.

For some, the end of mushroom season is a relief. It is a time to rest, to hibernate through the cold winter months, to divert energies to other pursuits—a job, perhaps a family, perhaps the birds of Costa Rica. Life, these mushroom hunters believe, continues after mushrooms. But just as the Aztecs believed that each night, when the sun set in the West, would be their last if they didn't offer a human sacrifice to the sun god, I too am certain that each November will signal the end of the last mushroom season. Searching for small ways to trick myself into believing otherwise, I postpone the inevitable. I mark on my calendar the series of winter lectures sponsored by the New York Mycological Society. I remember that in December I will attend the club's Christmas banquet, where dozens of dazzling dishes made from summer-fall collections await the hungry throngs: *Lepista* Stroganoff, creamed *abortivus* on pointed pumpernickel, paté of black trumpet soaked in whiskey. I will take all the winter courses I can find in microscopy and mushroom identification, offered at local universities and botanical gardens. And I will try my hand at the newly popular North American sport of mushroom cultivation.

For centuries in Europe and in the Orient, dozens of wild mushroom species have been cultivated and enjoyed by many mushroom-gathering, mushroom-loving people. Here, until recently, the only cultivated mushroom was the *Agaricus bisporus*, the species grown by the eight-billion-dollar-a-year industry and sold in supermarkets. To the general public, this bland, bleached species is the definitive mushroom. All others are toadstools to be assiduously avoided. To the respectable mushroom hunter,

Agaricus bisporus is only a poor imitation of a real mushroom, as natural to mycophagists as refined sugar is to health-food purists.

But suddenly, even mysteriously, dozens of wild mushrooms, collected and cultivated, are appearing on the menus of elegant restaurants and on the shelves of gourmet food stores. Small commercial farms that grow exotic species are springing up on both coasts. True mushroom hunters, who would recoil at the idea of buying a wild mushroom, are now enthusiastically learning to grow them. They are psychedelic farmers from the 1960s and 1970s who are eager to cultivate new and respectable markets. They are doctors with free access to a lifetime supply of petri dishes. They dream of riches. They dream of toy-filled basements with electrostatic filters and scanning electron microscopes. They dream of waking up in the morning to the smell of freshly grown mushrooms.

I order guides and catalogues. I follow the cultivation circuit from conference to workshop to a tour of a local shiitake farm. Cultivation, all growers say, is a very simple process. But they speak an alien language and, like the best chefs, are reluctant to divulge precise ingredients and proportions. Each grower uses just a slightly different mix. Sterilization can destroy beneficial bacteria, but unsterile conditions can produce penicillium, trichoderma, aspergillus, and other unwelcome pests.

As they talk, I dream. I am clearing out my clothes and scrubbing my closet as I have never scrubbed it before. I prepare my agar medium of potato dextrose and malt extract, add a dash of alfalfa and pea rinds, and transfer my sterile spores. In days, beautiful, cottony white mycelia appear in my petri dish. I am scouring the woods for logs, dragging them home and drilling them with holes. Then I plug them with shiitake spawn, and before I can say *Lentinus edodes*, trees filled with shiitake are crowding my backyard. I am queen of the shiitake forest. My throne is made of solid ash, my crown a garland of fresh mushrooms. "Just think," my friend Richard whispers through his sterilized face mask, "you never have to go outside again." His covered hands are reaching through the holes in a glove box into which he has transferred the growing mycelium, as if he were delivering a baby. "I only wish you could cultivate birds," he muses.

Slowly I awaken from my dream. Agriculture is the work of the devil. God had small regard for Cain's offering of the fruit of the earth. I am a hunter-gatherer, not a farmer. Life is only where the wild things are, and two ragged *Russulae* hiding in a forest grove are worth more to me than a canning jar with a bushel of the cultivated Japanese mushroom *enoke* sprouting from its mouth or a whole kingdom of shiitake. Let a hundred mushrooms bloom. Or even one.

As editor of the New York Mycological Society newsletter, I am buried beneath announcements about forays from local clubs around the country and the world. In Florida, Louisiana, Oregon, California, Yugoslavia, the Amazon, China, Japan, the Himalayas—why not, I think. I am not ready for winter. Just one more foray can't hurt. A magazine article will finance my trip; my neighbor will feed the cats. No one will even know I'm away.

There is a cold, misty drizzle in the air as I pull up to the Mt. Hood, Oregon, camp where a foray is being run by the Northwest Key Council, a consortium of mushroom hunters from Washington and Oregon dedicated to the pursuit of knowledge about local and regional fungi. "Key" refers not to a city, to a private washroom, nor to a social club, but to twenty-three homemade, color-coded dichotomous keys of mushroom genera in the area.

A dichotomous key is a long-standing tool of logic and

science used to give us the illusion that we are identifying, classifying, and organizing information that is ultimately unidentifiable, unclassifiable, and unorganizable. For example:

1. If you are holding a mushroom, proceed to (2).
   If you are holding another object, proceed to (3).
2. If the mushroom is purple, proceed to (7).
   If the mushroom is another color, proceed to (4).

And so on. Dichotomous keys are used in mushroom field guides and monographs to help sift through hundreds of closely related species.

A roaring fire warms the lodge; more than thirty other participants are already at work. Sprawled on the floor on blankets, sitting on stuffed wicker chairs, engrossed in field guides and surrounded by freshly picked mushrooms, they confer in low, reverential whispers. Looking around, I recognize no faces. The mushrooms look familiar, but I cannot name a single one. Then a familiar voice barrels across the room, and I begin to feel at home. It is Kit Scates, founder and guardian angel of the Northwest Key Council and a frequent visitor to our eastern forays.

"When in doubt, key it out," she is instructing a group of twenty students from Evergreen State College in Olympia, Washington, who are attending the foray as part of a sixteen-week, four-credit course on higher fungi. Kit is holding court behind a long, banquetlike table, surrounded by books, monographs, and mushrooms in varying states of decay. "We've got lots of mushrooms out West," she says, pointing to the large array before her, "but only a handful of professionals to identify them. And that's why we amateurs need to teach ourselves everything we can." She continues in a tone that falls somewhere between strident and Southern, reflecting her relentless drive and her South Carolina origins. In her franker moments, Kit makes up her own dichotomous key and divides the mushroom world into goons and gods: the former are the amateurs who bring in their collections on platters, and the gods are the professional mycologists who sit on Mount Olympus putting names on them. "But we goons," she has said repeatedly, "don't learn a thing that way." Now Kit turns to a bespectacled, befuddled gentleman and says, not unkindly, "You missed those scales on the cap. Go back and try it again."

When I first saw Kit in 1978, I admired her from afar, careful to stay out of her shadow as she lay on her stomach for hours photographing a single mushroom. Since then I have watched her, after a hard day of collecting, routinely work into the night with microscope, chemicals, and text. I have ridden in her red camper, stacked with camera equipment, mushroom drier, microscopes, and field guides, as she carried her self-help crusade from foray to foray. And I have tramped through the woods with her, stepping over my favorite edibles, always in search of the unknown. I can well imagine Kit staring down a rattlesnake that stands between her and an unidentified species of her favorite genus, *Ramaria*. "My driving 350 miles just to get a single mushroom identified must seem a little crazy," she once admitted to me. It did, but no crazier than the idea of spending almost every waking hour, as she has since her retirement from teaching, collecting, describing, identifying, photographing, lecturing, and writing about mushrooms.

My kids may be "grossed out" by the earthy smells that pervade our house. They may tell me that the refrigerator is full, all right, like in other houses, but not with food—ha ha. "You should meet Kit," I want to answer, but I know they would only reply, "Just because there's someone crazier than you doesn't mean you aren't crazy."

When I am with Kit I wonder if goon is a level that I can ever achieve. I run out of energy at the mere thought of nightless days and winterless months. I cannot follow her into infinity, in search of mushrooms forever. My close friends already complain that mine is a fair-weather friendship.

I am shivering from the cold, and I move toward the fire with a hot cup of coffee. Kit spies me from across the room. *"Here!"* she calls, instead of hello, with a big wave and a smile, "try one of these Western jobbies." My physical comfort can wait. I walk across the room and take the mushroom from her hand. It looks familiar, but I have never seen it before. *"Suillus,"* I say with authority. "That's the easy part," she answers, "now get the species." And she dumps into my lap a sheaf of pink, three-holed pages. At the top of the first page is the title: KEY TO SUILLUS OF THE PACIFIC NORTHWEST.

Afternoon turns into evening, the roaring fire to embers, and the only interruption from our work is dinner, where food is but a minor distraction. I become familiar with the names and faces of the West: *Boletus zelleri, Phaeocollybia olivacea,* Jim, Maggie, and Dick. Of the latter, I ask not where they live nor what they do but what genus they are working on. The outside world of crime and politics disappears, and there is nothing but mushrooms. It is a safe place, where law and order are taxonomic and the major issue of debate is "carpet sweeping," or the commercial harvesting of wild mushrooms. Chanterelles and matsutaki, the two most popular and prolific species out here, are picked and pickled or shipped fresh to Germany, where they are resold to restaurants and consumers or canned and shipped back to the United States for sale in specialty food shops. I hear too that planeloads of Japanese tourists appear in the Oregon woods from October through December and return to Japan the same day, picking enough matsutake to pay for the trip. Proponents and opponents of this commercial picking range all the way from those who support the practice as an exercise in free enterprise or as a means of support for unemployed loggers, to those who view commercial hunters as "feral" pigs and their crime worthy of punishment by *Amanita phalloides* poisoning.

"It's a crime!" I hear an angry voice behind me. A timid-looking woman from Seattle who has been quiet for most of the evening is engaged in heated debate with a group of people gathered around her. "They're depleting the forests. They're raping the land. Do you know that a single company last season collected over 210 tons of chanterelles? A single company!" "Overpicking causes fruiting failure," somebody else adds. "In Europe they've had to regulate the days, hours, and numbers of people who pick mushrooms. And that can happen here if we're not careful." Others add their voices: "Mushrooms nourish trees. Without them, there is ecological holocaust."

"*Nonsense!*" The room falls silent as Larry Stickney, the portly ex-president of the San Francisco Mycological Society, announces, "I can find no commandment that says"—he pauses—"thou shalt not pick and sell wild mushrooms." "Once a mushroom drops its spores"—another voice joins in—"its only job is to be picked and eaten." "Sounds to me more like a problem of etiquette," suggests Gary Lincoff, whose role as president of the North American Mycological Association requires him to deal with an issue he would much rather avoid, "than a problem of ecology. We're talking about less than a half-dozen species that happen to be popular edibles. There are still thousands of varieties out there doing their job, acting as saprophytes or trading nutrients with trees and shrubs. When they start harvesting tons of *Marasmius rotula*, that's when we have something to worry about."

Everybody is talking at once. The air is thick with charges and countercharges. "Regulate commercial picking with permits from the federal government." "Keep the government out of it. Let NAMA train and license commercial pickers." "Keep NAMA out of it. Leave them all alone." Off with their heads. My own head begins to nod. What has this to do with me? I come from the East, where, although there are chanterelles (in Maine and Vermont they are even considered common), they are more often like whales, sighted ever so rarely and worth a loud commotion from captain and crew. *Where there is plenty, there is plunder*, I think with a touch of righteousness.

Hunting mushrooms in the Northwest, I discover the next morning, is truly like living among the Brobdingnagians. Huge stands of Douglas fir and redwood tower above like gothic spires. The distances between single trees seem like the distances between New England cities. Giant cedars lie chest high where they fall, but it is still faster to climb over them than to walk around them. Mushrooms that I recognize and mushrooms that I have never seen appear like flocks of sheep among the leaves and pine needles. Brilliant scarlet fly agarics, large enough to shelter a full-size Alice. Chestnut-capped boletes, like stepping stones across a huge river. Orange chanterelles, as far as the eye can see, light our way through the forest.

I am like a prospector in this land of riches. I want to fall to my knees, throw my hat into the air, send for my family, and cry, "We're rich, we're rich." There is no gold more beautiful than that of the golden chanterelle.

Not Goldilocks. Not the flaxen-haired Rapunzel. Not the Golden Gate Bridge, rumored to be named for the California poppies that once covered the nearby hillsides. The western sun is bright, but it is only the reflection of a million chanterelles. And I want them all. Not to ship to Germany, I promise, but to wrap in wax paper, tie with ribbons, and hang as ornaments on Christmas trees. I will dry and freeze and can them. I will stew, sauté, simmer, bake, and roast them in heavy cream. I will throw them in the air like balloons. I will cover myself with them and float naked down the Nile. I have found the mushroom Garden of Eden and shall never again set foot outside it.

"We only take what we need." The voice startles me, perhaps the disembodied voice of childhood, upon hearing my shameful thoughts, catching me red-handed in the middle of a fantasy. But it is only Gary Menser, president of the fledgling Oregon Coast Mycological Society, author of *Hallucinogenic and Poisonous Mushroom Field Guide* and an active member of the Northwest Key Council. He stands above me, one leg astride a fallen tree, and I look up at his pale, Prince Valiant face, wondering if he has come to rescue me from the forest. Yes, the foray is ending, and he has come to lead me out. *Surely not so soon*, I think, *this is only the beginning.*

Later, he invites me to his home in Florence, Oregon. It's only a short distance from Mt. Hood, he promises. But there is a world of difference between the coast and the mountains. Different mushrooms. Different seasons. I hesitate a moment. Perhaps I should be getting home. But just one more day can't hurt. There are mountains to climb and rivers to cross and thousands of mushrooms still to be found.

The next afternoon, opening the door to Gary's Florence, Oregon, real estate office, I see a desk cluttered with open books. But they are mushroom field guides, not real estate codes. On the wall, instead of awards and certificates, are photographs of *Pholiota* clusters. Gary is on the telephone speaking in low, serious tones. When I hear the words "electrolyte balance" and "sed rate" instead of "mortgage" and "interest rate," I know he is not negotiating a closing. More likely, he is advising the Portland hospital, which he serves as a consultant, on its latest case of mushroom poisoning. He sees me, nods, and looks at his watch. It's three o'clock, too late for selling real estate anyway.

Gary guides me on a tour of his local mushroom fields. He used to work for the railroad, I learn, and spotted mushrooms along the tracks. Now he finds them on tracts, lawns, and wooded lots. We take a twenty-minute boat-ride to a pristine island wilderness across Siltcoos Lake, where he lives with his wife and two sons. Full-time mushroom hunting, Gary admits, can place a severe strain on the emotional and financial ties of family life. But obsession breeds invention, and he is convinced that he has found a way to turn a not-so-fruitful real estate business into a booming truffle estate business.

Did I know, he asks, that there are more truffles growing in the Pacific coastal states than in any area on earth comparable in size? Did I know that James Beard, the culinary authority, proclaimed the Oregon white truffle *(Tuber gibbosum)* equal in taste to the Italian white truffle *(Tuber magnatum)*, and that it is being sold in gourmet food stores all over the country? But wild truffles, he explains, are difficult to harvest. Like all mushrooms that fruit aboveground, these potatolike fruiting bodies depend on spore dispersal to reproduce; but they grow underground and cannot rely on wind, air currents, or the vision of hungry animals to spread them. Instead, truffles exude a strong and musty odor that attracts pigs, insects, and other underground or burrowing creatures.

The French, he tells me, have developed a method to cultivate their périgord truffle *(Tuber melanosporum)*, also known as the black diamond and about as expensive. "There is no reason why we can't grow our own truffles here, right in Oregon," he tells me. "The entire length of the coast is perfect for truffle farming. There's practically no frost; we have the right soil." Like chanterelles, boletes, and many other mushrooms, truffles are mycorrhizal, growing only in association with the roots of certain trees. Oak and filbert are two of their favorites, and there is no shortage of either in Oregon.

We are bouncing along in Gary's pickup truck past vast forest areas and empty fields. As we pass each nascent orchard, he names the owners, to whom he has sold truffle trees. He knows the soil content, acreage, and depth of each parcel, the microclimate, the pH factor, and the slope of the land as well as he knows his own family. I listen, spellbound, as he describes the long and complicated process.It takes five to seven years to grow from little acorn to mighty truffle, he tells me, and the first trees were planted only two years ago. But he is bursting with confidence, and as he talks the forests and hillsides are magically transformed into fertile truffle orchards with neat rows of truffle trees as far as the eye can see, black diamonds and white pearls glistening from under the soil, dollar signs hanging from the carefully pruned branches. My head is buzzing. Only eight dollars for one truffle tree. Two hundred and fifty trees per acre. That's only two thousand dollars, plus the cost of the land, for an acre of trees. My fingers are counting furiously. If an average acre yields a hundred pounds the first year and the wholesale price is $150 per pound, that's fifteen thousand dollars for only the first year . . . and the first acre . . .

What would it be like, I wonder, to be ruler of my

own truffle orchard, digging and planting my paradise? Dressed in red coat and jodhpurs, whip in hand, training truffle dogs to heed the early-morning bugle call of the truffle chase? But agriculture, many purists say, was the birth and death of civilization. I hear instead the mournful cry of a distant bugle. I am beginning to get cold and wet. It rains here too much for anything but mushrooms. The mail must be piled up outside my door like snow, and it is a long way home. I promise Gary I will come back, and perhaps one day soon I will, returning to see the bright neon sign as I drive down the highway: FLORENCE OREGON 5 MILES. TRUFFLE CAPITAL OF THE WORLD.

Before you know it, the coast of Oregon rounds a bend and turns into California. October segues into November and then December. I follow the yellow chanterelle as it beckons down Route #1, past giant cliffs and fields of brussels sprouts, stopping to visit friends and hunt mushrooms, all the way to L.A. But I am soon bored with endless days and have had my fill of Pacific sunsets. I long for dark, dreary afternoons. I miss the icy streets of February and the mushroomless woods covered with snow.

I drive faster. The road turns east into Texas, where I follow the signs that say HOUSTON FORAY THIS WAY followed by a handmade painted arrow. North of the city to the Big Thicket, once a three-and-a-half-million-acre wilderness, now reduced to eighty-four thousand acres by loggers and developers. Still, this "biological crossroads of North America," as it is advertised, is something to see and a just source of pride for Texans. I join a caravan of hunters, who scout from Big Sandy Creek to Jack Gore Baygall hunting for mushrooms among the sweet bay magnolia. A dark river sucks us deeper into the thicket past bald cypress and tupelo dripping with

Spanish moss, past eastern woodlands and desert cactus. A flash of color, a shrill sound, skins and skulls and eggs and footprints mark the goings-on of life and death. Why am I here? The chatter of mushroom hunters recedes as my own inner voices grow louder and I begin to dream.

Mushrooms are invading my house. They are climbing up the sides, covering the shingles, growing through the windows and down the chimney. They are in the telephone speaker, under the cushions of the couch. Mycelial tendrils reach out from under the crawlspace, squeezing the house in their fungal embrace.

The Texan foragers return, their baskets full, talking excitedly about the Louisiana foray only two weeks and two hundred miles away. I avert my eyes and decline their offer. I want to go home. There is comfort in the dead of winter.

I stand beside my car, ready to leave, thinking about my mother and my aunt, who used to drive me crazy as they stood at the doorway forever saying good-bye. Then I look into the back of the car. Strewn across the seat are dozens of books, dog-eared and stained, slides and cover-slips, scattered pages from a three-hole binder, a decaying bolete staining one page's description of *Boletus zelleri*. Wax paper bags filled with dried specimens, and twigs and branches covered with polypores cover the floor. In the front, five small potted truffle trees are lined up under the glove compartment. I get into the car and inhale deeply, trying without success to isolate and identify the different aromas. Pushing aside the large shiitake log on the seat next to me—a gift from a mushroom-growing friend in Watsonville, California—I drive toward home. The mushroom season is over.

But sometimes endings are beginnings. In a few hours the sun will rise again in the east. It is already January and only five more months until May.

Part II

FROM THE WOODS TO THE KITCHEN:

HINTS ON HUNTING, IDENTIFYING, COOKING, AND SURVIVING

CHAPTER 13

Introduction to the Field

A Sharp Eye, a Delicate Touch, and a Strong Nose

Most mushroom hunters go out into the woods expecting to find a dozen or so familiar edibles. In learning what these species are, you will also learn what they aren't and, in the process, learn to recognize dozens of other species that are poisonous, or that are inedible but harmless.

For some, identifying mushrooms turns out to be a far more challenging activity than finding them, and far more rewarding than eating them. It exercises the mind and creates the pleasant illusion that the world would be a manageable place if only we could put the right label on everything. To the newcomer, many mushrooms are indistinguishable, like so many ducks on a pond. But as you learn to tell a mallard from a decoy, you learn to tell a *Russula* from a stinkhorn. All you need is a sharp eye, a delicate touch, and a strong nose.

A mushroom will willingly answer a lot of your questions, but first you need to know what to ask: Where and how is it growing? On a log or on a tree? In a grassy meadow, under the leaves, or in the bathroom shower? Some mushrooms grow singly or in scattered groups; others grow in clusters, all attached to a single base. When you dig up a mushroom, be sure to get it all out and to examine the base: Is it straight or is it bulbous? Does it have a sac? When you turn mushrooms over, you will see that many have gills underneath the cap, while others have pores, teeth, or coral branches. Colors vary in tone and intensity. Mushrooms come in all shades of almost any color you can think of. Sometimes, but not always, color is a key to the mushroom's identity.

Feel the mushroom: Is it tough and leathery, fleshy, or fragile? Does it have a stem? Is the cap smooth, hairy, or slimy? Mushrooms give off an amazing variety of odors, resembling everything from nectar to burnt rubber. Like fingerprints, these characteristics of mushrooms are clues to proper identification.

When it comes to putting names on faces, it is all a matter of time, talent, and individual style. There are those maddening few for whom learning seems to be effortless. They see a mushroom once, hear the name, and they remember not only how to pronounce *Dasyscuphus virgineus* but will recognize this tiny white fairy cup of a mushroom every time they see it. Some people learn the characters of large families and then zero in on the genus and species; others learn the mushrooms one at a time and don't worry about family relationships. Some people remember Latin names the way a baseball buff remembers batting averages. Then there are those like me who can hear the name of a mushroom forty-two times, know every tuft, wart, and fibril on its cap and stem, tell you whether its cuticle is cellular or filamentous, remember how many and what shape the microscopic cystidia are, and still ask, "What is it?"

If you want to learn more than a handful of species, a field guide is essential. Even twenty-year veterans keep one in their back pockets. There are probably a hundred in English alone, ranging from small local and regional guides to books that cover North America. No two books are alike in quality, selection of species, or organization. Some are illustrated with lush colored plates; others rely on a clear, precise text and limit themselves to black and white drawings or photographs. Some are universally respected; others are totally useless. Everyone has their favorites, and even those people who own thirty field guides usually rely most heavily on one or two. On p. 265 I have listed the books that seem most popular among, and useful for, mushroom hunters.

Apart from buying books, mushroom hunting is not an expensive activity. All you need is a basket, a box of wax paper or some wax paper bags, a knife, a 10x hand lens, a compass, insect repellent, index cards, lunch, and of course your favorite field guide. Pick fresh specimens, and try to find them at different stages of development. On one side of an index card, note the habitat (lawn, log, tree, kind of tree if you know it, and so on). On the other side, when you get home, you will want to place a cap gill-side down, cover it with a glass, and take a spore print. Spore color is very important in the identification of most gilled mushrooms. And remember to wrap each species separately in wax paper. Sometimes you might want to stop and actually use your field guide in the field. Ideally, this patient and efficient style of collecting will make your task of sorting and identifying much easier.

I know of few collectors who follow their own advice, however, and more often than not I find myself forgetting everything but lunch.

The Gilled Mushrooms

These are what most of us picture when we say the word *mushroom*. They have a stalk and a rounded cap

Mushroom with gills clearly evident
on underside of cap (*Stropharia rugosoannulata*)

with gills underneath. Spores develop on these bladelike
gills, which radiate from the stalk to the edge of the cap.

Gilled mushrooms come in a dazzling variety of sizes
and colors and an infinite variety of characteristics that
are clues to their identification: central and off-center
stalks; gills that are close, distant, smooth, or serrated;
caps that are velvety, slimy, scaly, or fuzzy; spore colors
that are white, pink, brown, or purple-black. Some grow
on the ground; others grow on wood. Some grow singly;
others grow scattered or in clusters. Most of the mushrooms found in woods and on lawns are gilled. They include some of the best common edibles (the honeys, ble-

wits, parasols, and meadow mushrooms) as well as some of the deadliest killers (the *Amanitae* and *Galerinae*).

Boletes

With over two hundred species in North America, this large family of mushrooms, Boletaceae, is easy to recognize. Boletes often resemble gilled mushrooms from the top, but when you turn them over you will notice a spongy bottom or pored surface instead, which may be white, gray, yellow, orange, red, or brown.

Boletes grow in mycorrhizal, or symbiotic, association with the roots of many trees, and some grow under only one kind of tree such as ash, white pine, or larch. By noticing this, you can learn about both trees and mushrooms. Many boletes will turn blue when they are bruised.

Boletes
(*Leccinum scabrum*)

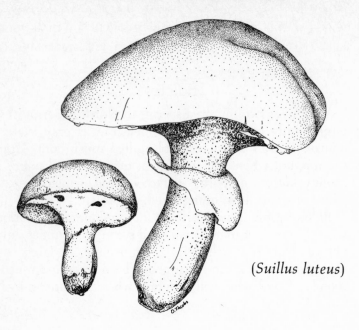

(*Suillus luteus*)

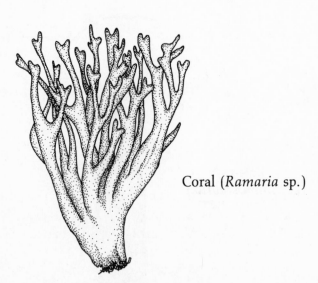

Coral (*Ramaria* sp.)

Corals

Many members of this mushroom family, Clavari-
aceae, truly resemble underwater coral. They usually come
club-shaped or branched and in many bright colors, from
white to yellow, pink, orange-red, amethyst. Sometimes
they will cover the ground in late summer or fall, particularly favoring conifer woods. Others resemble cauliflower or heads of lettuce. Most coral mushrooms are
edible. A few, like *Sparassis crispa* and *Sparassis radi-
cata*, are choice.

Discomycetes

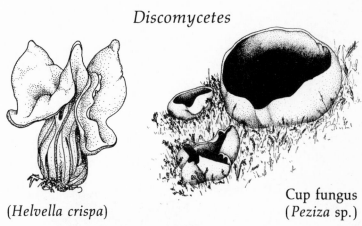

(*Helvella crispa*)

Cup fungus
(*Peziza* sp.)

Cup Fungi

Turning over a rotten log on a wet spring day will
often reveal a tiny orange or scarlet mushroom shaped
like a cup. Appropriately named cup fungi, these brightly
colored species are part of a class, consisting of many
families and orders, called Discomycetes, which contains
all the fungi resembling cups or saucers, spoons, sponges,
saddles, brains, tongues, urns, or fans—including the
highly esteemed morel and truffle.

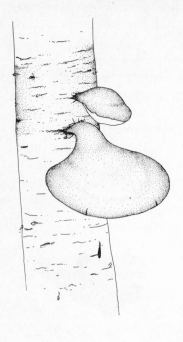

Polypore
(*Piptoporus betulinus*)

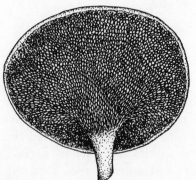

Polypore showing pores
on the underside of the cap
(*Favolus lalveolaris*)

Polypores

Even on dry days and in the dead of winter, these mushrooms will cover trees and stumps with fungal shelves. *Polypore* means "many pores." If you turn over one of the mushrooms in this very large and diverse group, you will see tiny holes—hexagonal, round, or mazelike—under the cap.

Some polypores are edible and delicious. Many are tough and leathery. They can be virulent parasites on living trees or they can serve an important function as saprophytes helping to decay dead wood.

In many cultures and for many centuries, certain polypores have been used as tinderboxes, perfumes, dyes, and as medicines and tonics.

Puffballs and Earthstars

One of the most common groups of mushrooms, puffballs grow throughout the summer and fall in all parts of the country, in grassy areas and on logs. Sometimes they are large, round, and white like a soccer ball; other times they grow like small prickly pears in dense clusters. Puffballs and earthstars are of the class Gasteromycetes, a word that means "stomach mushroom"; their spores mature while completely enclosed in and protected by a surrounding "skin." Their various methods of spore dispersal help determine the particular genus. Members of the genus *Lycoperdon*, for example, release their spores through a tiny hole in the top; in the genus *Calvatia*, the surface of the mushroom cracks and peels away.

Puffballs are known for their therapeutic use as styptics and surgical dressings. Many people, from American Indians to English barbers, have used puffballs to control

Puffball (*Calvatia gigantea*)

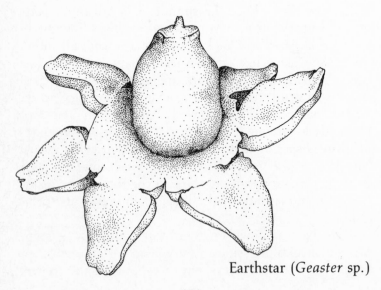

Earthstar (*Geaster* sp.)

nosebleeds and to stop bleeding after surgery. The fumes, possessing properties of chloroform, have also been used effectively as anesthetics.

Earthstars, which like puffballs are members of the order *Lycoperdales*, are small fungi that resemble flying saucers. They are shaped like a ball when young; then the surface splits open, releasing the spores through the top, and the pieces curve back, forming four or more arms that resemble a star. Growing mostly in sandy soil, earthstars are distributed throughout North America. Like puffballs, they have been used by widely varying cultures as hemostatic agents and as antiinflammatory and lung and throat tonics.

Stinkhorns

Your nose will probably lead you to these strong-smelling mushrooms before you ever catch sight of them. But when you do, you will discover some of the most colorful, oddly shaped fungi in the forest. The stinkhorns, which are of the order Phallales, have evolved a unique means of spore dispersal. The spores are embedded in a slimy green substance that smells of decaying flesh. The odor draws flies and other insects, which remove the slime—and also the spores—with their feet. Stinkhorns first appear as eggs that resemble puffballs or *Amanita* eggs. As it matures, the egg opens by expansion from within, and fanciful shapes develop. Stinkhorns are exotic and erotic, largely southern in their habitat. Some species will actually grow indoors if you place the egg on wet paper towels and cover it with a glass bowl. In China, the egg of the genus *Dictyophora* is eaten as a great delicacy and was served to President Nixon on his state visit.

Stinkhorns

(Dictyophora duplicata)

(Pseuducolus schellenbergii)

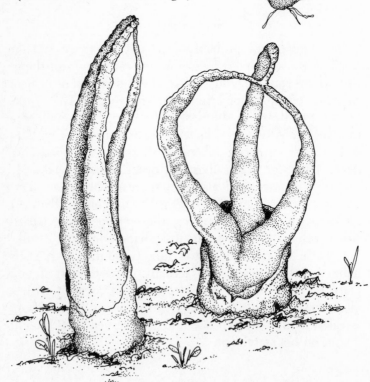

Tooth Fungi

It may seem like Christmas in September when you are in the woods and walk smack into a tree decorated with large clusters of glistening white icicles. But the tree is more likely to be an oak, maple, or beech than a fir or spruce, and the cluster of icicles is a mushroom called *Hericium*.

Members of a large family of mushrooms called *Hydnaceae*, the genera *Hericium*, *Dentinum*, and *Hydnum* produce their spores on long spines or teeth that hang down toward the ground. Although not as common as boletes and polypores, these tooth fungi are just as easy to recognize. Unlike any other mushroom, some, like the *Hericium*, grow on logs, stumps, and living trees, and thus they are noticeable from a distance. The smaller *Dentinum* often grows on the ground with caps of many colors. Although none of the tooth fungi are known to be poisonous, many are too tough and bitter to eat. Several species of *Hericium* and *Dentinum* are edible and choice.

Tooth Fungus
(*Hericium erinaceus*)

CHAPTER 14

Twenty Edibles

THERE ARE THOUSANDS of species of wild mushrooms in North America. A few hundred of these are known to be edible. Most people, however, who go out looking for mushrooms are satisfied with the dozen or so that they know like the back of a silver spoon. Although few people would choose the same dozen, no one's list would omit the morel, the chanterelle, and the cep, three mushrooms that are also sold—dried, canned, or fresh—in food stores and markets around the world.

Hunting wild mushrooms to eat is a popular pastime that dates back at least to ancient Rome. In France, Germany, and Italy it is a weekend family activity, as well as the source of more than a few border disputes. For centuries, peasants in Russia and Poland have relied on dried and pickled fungi to help them through the severe northern winters. In the Orient, the cultivation of mushrooms has been a thriving industry for centuries.

The hunting of mushrooms in North America is a much more recent development. Our Anglo-Saxon mycophobic heritage, in which mushrooms or "toadstools" are viewed with fear and distaste, prevails. In North America, even some professional mycologists express a certain distaste for eating mushrooms and for those of us who follow such an idle pursuit. Many North Americans who are mushroom hunters are descended from Italian, German, and East European families in which the parents and grandparents told stories of mushroom hunting or took their children for walks in the woods, pointing out *borovik*, *Pfifferling*, or *lapacentro buono*. Other mushroom hunters are naturalists, wild-food enthusiasts, gourmet cooks, gardeners, birdwatchers, or entomologists who stumbled on mushrooms while hot on the trail of something else. However, many of them do not dare to venture beyond the aisles of the foodstores for edible fungi. (When I worked at the Bronx Zoo, I conquered my fear of snakes by handling a resident six-foot boa constrictor, looking into his eyes and trusting him enough to let him wrap around me. Then one day in the woods I came upon a small garter snake lazing under a tree. I didn't get closer than six feet before I jumped and ran. This, after all, was the wild!)

For many Americans, then, eating wild mushrooms is still a risky business. For the rest of us, it is challenging, frustrating, and time-consuming, but the rewards are many, and by following a few simple rules the risks can be reduced to almost zero.

1. Only eat a mushroom you can positively identify (as edible, of course). There is no way to tell a poisonous species from an edible one except to learn them both. No silver spoons, blackened onions, or tarot cards. You should be able to learn, without much trouble, a dozen or so easily recognizable good edibles and the small number of deadly toxic species. Use your eyes, your field guides, and other amateurs whom you trust to enhance your knowledge.

2. *Be patient and don't cut corners.* Pick the whole mushroom; identification is often determined by the base—the part that is sometimes underground. Take a spore print when you aren't absolutely certain. It will often lead to positive identification, especially with gilled mushrooms. Separate the edible species in your basket from those that you know to be inedible and from those that you can't identify, and when you get home, go through the collection again—sometimes two similar but different species can get mixed up in the basket.

3. *Even after you have positively identified a mushroom as edible, eat only a small amount the first time.* Some people have an adverse reaction to certain mushrooms; it's usually mild but can be uncomfortable and is worth avoiding.

4. *Be sure that you know the local flora where you are hunting.* If you live in New York and are visiting California, or vice versa, double-check your identifications. Species can vary from region to region, and some are unique to a particular area. It has been suggested that most poisonings in the United States take place because of this kind of mistake. Not long ago, a family of fourteen Laotians was seriously poisoned in California by a deadly *Amanita* species. Upon interviewing the family, hospital authorities discovered that this was a mushroom that they did not have at home but that looked just like a perfectly safe edible that they did have. A few species, then, are toxic in one region and harmless in another.

5. *Only eat firm, fresh, young mushrooms.* As they age, mushrooms decay rapidly, sometimes causing toxic reactions. They also don't taste as good.

6. *Cut into mushrooms to check them for insect holes and other evidence of living creatures.* They probably won't hurt you, but it is no more pleasant to find a grub in your mushroom soup than it is to find half a worm in your apple.

7. *To be on the safe side, cook all mushrooms thoroughly.* Although some can be eaten raw without harm, many delicious species, like the honey mushroom and many boletes, contain toxins that are easily destroyed by proper cooking. Several minutes of sautéeing or parboiling over a medium-high flame is sufficient.

8. *Drink alcohol moderately when you taste any mushroom, and not at all with a member of the genus* Coprinus. Many field guides advise you not to drink liquor at all when you eat wild mushrooms. A few species, like *Coprinus atramentarius,* may cause an unpleasant reaction if you do. I have never had any such problems but would suggest that you excercise caution in this area.

9. *In the field, wrap your mushrooms in wax paper or wax paper bags.* Plastic will cause them to decay more rapidly. To preserve them until cooking, keep them in the refrigerator.

Mushrooms are excellent assimilators, adapting to, even enhancing, almost any culinary environment that they find themselves in (with the possible exception of Jell-O and chocolate-chip cookies): soups, soufflés, stews, vegetable casseroles, sauces, omelettes, ragouts, pasta, breads, and cheeses. They may also be eaten alone as finely chopped duxelles, or they may be sautéed, pickled, or broiled. Many are interchangeable, and recipes often call simply for "½ lb. mushrooms." But just as they do in the field, wild mushrooms also defy easy categorizing in the kitchen. In general, a more delicately flavored mushroom will do best in a chicken, veal, or other light dish, while stronger-tasting mushrooms can take more highly seasoned meats and sauces. Every mushroom has an individual taste, texture, color, and aroma that interacts differently with different dishes. Experimenting with wild species has been the joy of mushroom cookery for generations.

Most mycophagists believe that mushrooms are more desirable and tastier unwashed. You should cut and clean off most of the dirt in the field; at home, you can wipe them with a damp paper towel or a soft brush. But I would rather eat a few small bugs or a few grains of dirt than lose the flavor and would rather not think at all about dogs in city parks, air pollution, or lead from passing cars. There are, of course, those who fervently disagree, arguing that washing is necessary and, in all but a few cases, does little to destroy the flavor of mushrooms. They suggest that if you wash them well, drain them in a colander gill-side down, put them in a paper-towel-lined bowl, and cover them with more paper and refrigerate them, the water will evaporate and bring to life even the most "unmarvelous mushrooms."

The first time you cook a mushroom, make it a one-species sautéed dish. Half the fun in mushroom cookery is experimenting, and this will give you the chance to experience your find in all its glorious essence. Start over a low flame with some butter and a small amount of oil to prevent burning. Some species, like the chicken mush-room, are profligate butter soakers. They soon begin to dry out, and the butter keeps disappearing no matter how much you add. These mushrooms need a very low, slow flame and may be best covered. Others will turn golden before your eyes—brown if you turn away for a sec-ond—and then will shrivel and sizzle right out of the pan. So remove them right away—don't answer the phone while you are sautéeing mushrooms. After a while, you will become familiar with each species' habits in frying pans, and you will decide for yourself how much salt and pepper to use, whether to add garlic or shallots, or dip them in sour cream, or add them to a spaghetti sauce, or just put them on toast points and serve them to your guests.

Sometimes you will collect more mushrooms than you can use in a single meal and will want to preserve them. Drying, freezing after first lightly sautéeing or parboil-ing, and pickling are the three usual ways to keep mush-rooms. Some, you will discover, like morels and boletes, are enhanced by drying. Others, like the meadow mush-room, are better frozen. Depending on the amount of water in the mushroom and its fleshiness, it will take anywhere from a few hours to a few days to dry—placed either out on a table in the sun, or on a screen or drying rack in a gas oven with the pilot light on.

In the next section, I will describe twenty good edi-bles, followed by suggestions for preserving and cooking, and selected favorite recipes. Although it should be help-ful in identification, this section is not intended to serve as a field guide. For that purpose, I have included a list of six suggested books on page 265. Be sure to check at least one, better two, for specific details of description, such as habitat, spore color, and toxic look-alikes. Con-tributed by mycophagists and mushroom societies around the country, the recipes are not intended to be followed slavishly. You should vary amounts and ingredients according to your taste. As you become familiar with the individual mushrooms, you will be inventing your own recipes.

Taste is subjective, but the section does include the best-known edibles (morels, ceps, chanterelles); the three easiest to recognize (shaggy mane, hen-of-the-woods, the chicken mushroom); the most plentiful (honey, meadow mushroom); the favorites of others (the aborted *Entoloma*, the blewit); and my favorites (the parasol and the American matsutake). These mushrooms have little in common beyond their edibility. They are gilled and non-gilled; they grow on wood and on the ground, in forests, on lawns, in all seasons, and many of them in all parts of the country. I have also included the shiitake, which grows wild in Japan and is cultivated in the United States. I hope that its reputation and popularity, along with those of other cultivated mushrooms, will attract the food-store hunter out onto the lawns and into the woods, where the "real" mushrooms are.

The Aborted *Entoloma* (*Entoloma abortivum*)

These weird white masses that at first glance resemble wrinkled puffballs are found in the fall, growing abundantly on the ground and on or near stumps or rotten wood. True to their name, what they really are is an aborted species of *Entoloma*, having been invaded by the mycelium of the honey mushroom. You can often find these white balls growing next to a healthy, normal *Entoloma abortivum*, which is also called *abortivum* even though it is not aborted. It is a gray-capped, white-stalked, more ordinary-looking mushroom. Although both forms are edible, it is safer to stick to the easily recognized aborted version and leave the healthy one alone—there are toxic *Entolomae* that have gray caps and are difficult to distinguish from *abortivum*. Be sure to cut open the white *abortivum* before you eat it. It will have marbly pinkish veins inside and should be firm, not mushy.

This mushroom can grow in large quantities and is best preserved by being sautéed lightly and then frozen. It has a lovely, delicate flavor, and I have used it frequently in veal and chicken dishes with cream sauce.

Abortivum Soufflé (entrée)
FROM BILL WILLIAMS

3 tablespoons butter
3 tablespoons flour
1 cup hot milk
5 eggs, separated
¼ pound Swiss cheese, grated

¾ cup finely chopped *abortivum*, lightly sautéed
1 tablespoon grated Parmesan cheese
Salt and pepper to taste

Preheat oven to 375°F. Butter a 1½-quart soufflé dish and sprinkle with Parmesan cheese.

In a medium saucepan, melt butter and add flour. Cook, stirring, until bubbly and golden, about 2 minutes.

Add hot milk and whisk vigorously until well blended and smooth. Continue to cook, stirring constantly, 1–2 minutes. Add salt and pepper and remove from heat.

In a separate dish, beat 5 egg whites until foamy. Add pinch of salt and continue to beat until egg whites are stiff but not dry.

Entoloma
abortivum

Beat 3 of the egg yolks into the sauce. Add the mushrooms and the grated Swiss cheese. Stir about ¼ of the egg whites into the sauce. Fold in the remainder of the egg whites gently but thoroughly. Sprinkle cheese on top.

Spoon into the prepared dish and bake 35–40 minutes or until puffed and golden. SERVES 4.

American Matsutake *(Armillaria ponderosa)*

A local cousin of the Japanese *Tricholoma matsutake*, the North American species is sold fresh here in Japanese food stores and commands quite a hefty price. It is avidly pursued by amateurs in the Northwest; it is also a favorite of commercial hunters, who collect it by the ton, raking up the ground to find the firm young buttons, thus disturbing the soil and causing mycological temperatures to rise. Growing generally under conifers or in sandy soil from August to November, the matsutake is also common in Colorado; it is a rare treasure back East.

This robust, thick-fleshed mushroom is rewarding to

learn about. Like many of the *Amanitae*, it has a white cap, white gills, a white spore print, and a ring. But the similarity ends there. The reddish-brown scales on the cap and stem, the gills that turn brown when they are bruised, and the spicy, fragrant odor make this desirable fungus easy to distinguish from the *Amanita*.

Some devotees of this mushroom believe that because of its strong flavor it is too intense to use as a separate side dish. They prefer it in omelettes, with rice, or thinly sliced, floating on top of Japanese broth.

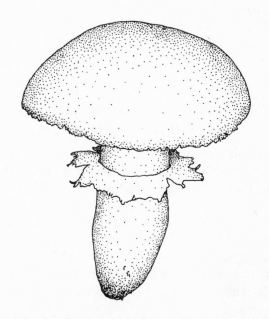

American Matsutake (*Armillaria ponderosa*)

Classic Matsutake (appetizer)
FROM ANDREW WEIL AND PEONY MUNGER

4 large American
matsutake mushrooms

Soy sauce to taste
Salt to taste

Slice the perfect mushroom specimens lengthwise through cap and stem, ⅛″ thick. Prepare a charcoal grill or hibachi, and when the coals are ready, place the slices on the grill, turning them with chopsticks or other utensil until they begin to brown.

Sprinkle with salt, and pass the slices as they are ready to waiting guests, who may wish to dip them in a little soy sauce and drink warm sake as an accompaniment.

Shiitake is a good substitute for this dish, but without stems.   SERVES 4.

Black Trumpet (*Craterellus fallax* or *Craterellus cornucopioides*)

This small, delicate, vase-shaped mushroom is related to the chanterelle, although it is far more fragile. The inside of the cap is black, and the outside is grayish. The black trumpet has a fruity odor. It grows across North America from July to November, hidden in the leaves under oak, beech, or other deciduous trees. The French name, *trompette du mort*, refers to the funereal colors of the mushroom rather than to its impact on the eater, for the black trumpet is one of the most eagerly sought-after edibles around.

The flavor of this mushroom is greatly enhanced by drying it and rehydrating it in cream, wine, or even water, but be sure to bring home a large collection. This is a

Black Trumpet (*Craterellus cornucopioides*)

small mushroom, and when dried it shrivels up to next to nothing. It is excellent with eggs, in casseroles, and in paté; some people use it as a truffle substitute.

Craterellus Dip (appetizer)
FROM PATRICK LENNON OF THE BOSTON MYCOLOGICAL SOCIETY

¼–½ cup dried black trumpets, rehydrated in milk

¼ teaspoon salt

8 ounces cream cheese

½ cup heavy cream

¼ teaspoon salt

Pepper to taste

Soak the mushrooms in milk for about 1 hour or until soft. Heat briefly and drain.

Mix the cream cheese and the heavy cream. Add the softened mushrooms. Add salt and pepper, and stir well.

Serve on small breads or crackers. SERVES 4.

Blewit *(Lepista nuda* or *Clitocybe nuda)*

Formerly a *Tricholoma*, now a *Clitocybe* to some and a *Lepista* to others, this poor mushroom has been passed around from genus to genus like an unwanted foster child. To foragers seeking mushrooms for the kitchen, it is very wanted indeed. It is found across the United States, hiding under fall or early winter leaf litter or in garden mulch. The first one is always the hardest to spot, but where there is one, there are usually a dozen or more. With a grayish lilac cap, lavender gills, and pinkish buff spores, the blewit has no dangerous look-alikes. As often as not, however, joy turns to despair when a bountiful harvest of blewits turns out to be the similar-appearing *Cortinarius albo-violaceus*. But a quick look will distinguish the rusty brown gills and spore print of the harmless but not very tasty *Cortinarius* from its more desirable look-alike.

The blewit has a delicate, earthy flavor. It is excellent when cooked under the broiler with sour cream or with a light cheese. The blewit will keep well if dried or frozen.

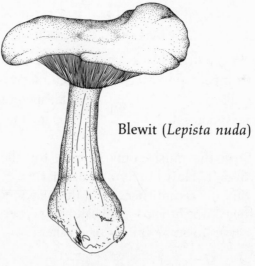

Blewit (*Lepista nuda*)

Creamed Blewits (side dish)

2 tablespoons butter
1 tablespoon finely
  chopped shallots
1¼ pound blewits,
  thinly sliced

Juice of one lemon
3 tablespoons wine
¾ cup heavy cream
Salt and pepper to taste

Melt the butter in a saucepan and add the shallots. Cook, stirring, about 3 minutes, adding the mushrooms and lemon juice. Sprinkle with salt and pepper and cook, stirring often, until most of the liquid evaporates.

Add the wine, stirring briefly. Add the heavy cream, stir, and bring to a boil. Serve hot. SERVES 4.

Chanterelle *(Cantharellus cibarius)*

Whenever the subject of eating wild mushrooms comes up, this orange-fluted mushroom is one of the first to make mouths water. The chanterelle is a prized edible in Europe, where its many seekers have created a scarcity. Commercial harvesters are collecting it by the ton in Maine, California, and the Pacific Northwest, often for shipment overseas.

There are several choice species of chanterelles, but it is *Cantharellus cibarius* that is the best known and most popular. There are few sights more tantalizing than a woodland floor carpeted with scores of this vase-shaped orange mushroom.

In beginning mushroom courses, the chanterelle is usually presented as one of the easiest mushrooms to recognize. Still, it has several look-alikes; one of them is poisonous, and it does take some care to tell them apart.

Chanterelle
(*Cantharellus cibarius*)

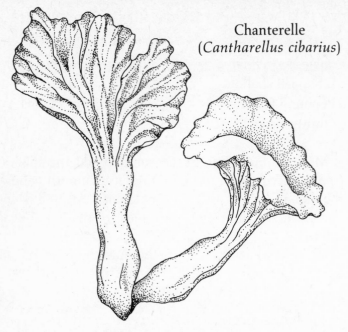

The chanterelle is distinguished from its look-alikes by the presence of blunt ridges—they are not really gills—with forked veins running down the cap and onto the stem.

The poisonous jack o'lantern *(Omphalotus olearius)* has sharp, knife-edged gills. It is a fall rather than a summer mushroom, it grows on wood rather than the ground, and it grows in large clusters rather than singly or in scattered groups. Despite these clear differences, there are more reported poisoning cases in the East resulting from confusion between these two mushrooms than any others.

Chanterelles are firm, fleshy mushrooms with a strong fruity aroma that often resembles apricot. Although it is best to cook all fresh mushrooms as soon after collecting them as possible, chanterelles can be kept for a week if they are well refrigerated. And although no one will disagree about their edibility, there is little agreement regarding how they are best cooked. Some say they absolutely need a long, slow sauté over a low fire; I have also heard that one or two minutes over a higher flame until the mushrooms are almost crisp is best. Some people prefer them as a side dish, untainted by other tastes, while others cannot think of a better way to stuff Cornish game hens or make rice pilaf than by using chanterelles.

Chanterelles are excellent fresh, of course; they can also be sautéed and frozen. As for drying, it seems that the varieties on the West Coast dry well, while our East Coast varieties, it is said, become a little leathery upon rehydration.

Braised Chanterelles (side dish)
FROM LARRY STICKNEY OF THE SAN FRANCISCO MYCOLOGICAL SOCIETY

2 pounds fresh
   chanterelles, sliced or
   cut in quarters
1 cup hot water
2 teaspoons chicken stock
3 tablespoons butter,
   divided

2 teaspoons lemon juice
4–5 shallots, finely
   chopped
¼ cup sherry
Dash of cayenne
Salt and pepper to taste

Preheat over to 350°F.

Place the hot water, 2 Tbs. butter, the chicken stock, and the lemon juice in a saucepan. Add the mushrooms and simmer for 10 minutes.

Remove the mushrooms, and reduce the liquid to 1 cup.

Sauté the shallots in remaining butter until they are transparent. Place the stewed mushroom slices in a baking dish with a cover. Add the shallots, the reduced liquid, the sherry, and the cayenne.

Cover the dish, and bake for 30 minutes or until tender. Check occasionally, turning the mushrooms in their braising liquid.

Correct the seasoning with salt and pepper. This is an especially suitable accompaniment for broiled steaks or beef roasts. SERVES 4.

Ray La Sala's Chanterelles (side dish)

Two cups of julienned
  chanterelles
2 tablespoons minced
  onions
1 tablespoon butter

1–2 sprigs fresh coriander
  leaves (optional)
1 apricot, minced fresh
  or dried
Black pepper

Sauté the onions in the butter about 5 minutes, until they begin to soften and become translucent. If you use dried apricot, soften in butter. Add the mushrooms, and cook until nearly done, about 5 minutes. Add the (optional) coriander leaves and the fresh apricot. Season with pepper. SERVES 4.

Chicken Mushroom (*Laetiporus sulphureus*)

This fleshy, colorful polypore is plentiful, popular, and easy to spot. Growing on stumps, logs, and living trees, its large overlapping shelves of orange and yellow always remind me of giant Halloween candy corn. The chicken mushroom, or sulphur shelf, is a wound parasite. Its

Chicken Mushroom (*Laetiporus sulphureus*)

mycelium enters a tree through an opening caused by lightning, axe, or woodpecker and penetrates to the heartwood, releasing enzymes to digest the cellulose, thus causing the wood to rot. It is known to damage wooden boats and to be a major cause of dry rot.

The sulphur shelf grows on many kinds of wood, but in the East I have found it mostly on oak. It grows from May to November in all parts of the country. One tree may provide over twenty pounds. All of it *may* be edible, but the best parts to eat are the tender young tips. The mushroom should be moist—almost slimy, according to some purists—when it is picked. The taste should be soft and lemony; if it is chalky, don't eat it, no matter how beautiful and how tempting it looks. As the mushroom ages it toughens and is frequently distasteful. In the East this is one of the safest edibles around, with no look-alikes. It is rarely eaten in California, where it grows on eucalyptus trees, or in the Pacific Northwest. Eat it in moderate amounts the first time you try it, since it is reported to have occasionally caused swollen lips.

Some say the flavor of this mushroom resembles chicken; I don't agree, although it is used often enough in recipes calling for chicken, and it is especially tasty in stir-fry Chinese dishes. It is good sautéed, either alone or dipped in flour, egg, and bread crumbs. It can also be dipped in pancake batter and deep-fried. When sautéeing, be sure to cook the mushroom very slowly over a low flame; it soaks up butter quickly. The chicken mushroom is excellent pickled and can be frozen after sautéeing. It is not good dried.

Chinese-style *Laetiporus Sulphureus* (vegetable)
FROM RICHARD KOEPPEL

2 cups tender tips of young mushroom cut into slices or bite-size pieces
¼ cup peanut oil (or enough to keep mushroom from drying out)
1 tablespoon Hoisin sauce
1 teaspoon powdered ginger
2 tablespoons chopped Chinese chives
1 tablespoon chopped fresh coriander (cilentro) leaves

Heat peanut oil and stir-fry mushrooms. Add Hoisin sauce and powdered ginger and continue to stir-fry about 5–10 minutes or until it is uniformly glazed. Sprinkle with Chinese chives and coriander leaves. Serve hot.   SERVES 4.

Chicken Sulfureus with Spinach (entrée)
From Edwina Chin of
the Boston Mycological Society

1 chicken breast, boned and sliced bite size
1 teaspoon light soy sauce
1 teaspoon sherry
1 teaspoon cornstarch
4 tablespoons oil
1 teaspoon salt
1 cup *L. sulfureus* sliced bite size
1 tablespoon tofu, mashed
½ teaspoon sugar
½ teaspoon salt
½ cup chicken stock
1 10-ounce package of fresh spinach,
    washed and cut into small pieces

Combine chicken, soy sauce, sherry, and cornstarch in a bowl. Let stand 10 minutes.

Meanwhile, heat 1 tablespoon oil and ¼ teaspoon salt in skillet and sauté mushrooms until done (about 10 minutes). *L. sulfureus* cooks slowly and you may need to add more oil. Remove and set aside.

Prepare tofu mixture by mixing it with sugar, ½ teaspoon salt, and stock.

In deep kettle, heat 1 tablespoon oil and ¼ teaspoon salt. Add spinach, 2 tablespoons bean mixture, and stir until just wilted. Remove to platter.

In skillet, heat 2 tablespoons oil and stir-fry chicken until it has lost its pink color. Add tofu mixture and mushrooms. Stir-fry 2 minutes longer. Thicken gravy if necessary with a little cornstarch and water mixture. Serve over spinach on platter.   SERVES 2.

Fairy-Ring Mushroom *(Marasmius oreades)*

Although many species of mushrooms grow in fairy rings, this small, tan-capped one alone claims the name. For centuries, alternating rings of dark green grass and brown areas surrounded by a circle of mushrooms attracted the curious and inspired explanations that they were caused by dragons' breath, lightning bolts, the dancing feet of fairies, or the passing by of witches on Walpurgis Night. Later, less-fanciful minds insisted they were caused by the mycelia of mushrooms, perennially spreading out and seeking nourishment, depleting yearly the nutrients in each succeeding zone of grass. Fairy rings are astounding phenomena, growing sometimes for hundreds of feet and for several hundred years.

The fairy-ring *Marasmius* is a small, buff, innocuous mushroom with whitish gills and a white spore print. It grows on grass, not always in fairy rings but almost always in large congregations. As it grows, a knob develops in the center of the cap and the edges of the cap start to turn up. At first glance, this mushroom looks like many other small, buff species, but it has an unusual feature that sets it apart: It has a pliant stem. After it dries out from age or exposure to the sun, the mushroom will revive after a rain and spring up in the grass as if it were new. If you take a handful of dryish specimens and place them in water, they will do the same. The fairy-ring mushroom grows throughout North America from May to September and year-round in California, where I have found it in December and February covering lawns in Hollywood, Beverly Hills, and other star-studded habitats.

There is another small whitish mushroom that may also grow in fairy rings. It is called *Clitocybe dealbata* and contains the toxin muscarine, which causes sweating, chills, and other unpleasant symptoms. This mushroom

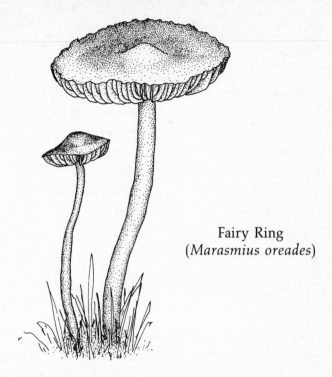

Fairy Ring
(*Marasmius oreades*)

is distinguished from the *Marasmius* largely by its de-current gills, extending partially down the stalk.

Many people find the *Marasmius* an excellent edible. It is good fresh, sautéed in eggs, or combined with cream and turned into a spaghetti sauce. Kept dried in covered jars, it will last forever, and it can be reconstituted in a broth with white vermouth. For a robust steak sauce, the mushroom should be cooked in butter and shallots, with the juice of the steak added. Since I find these mush-rooms bland, I once tried them in a cookie recipe. But while the cookies were excellent, I hardly tasted the mushrooms.

However you cook or preserve them, be sure to re-move the stems—they are often tough and rubbery.

Fresh Marasmius Bisque
FROM GREG WRIGHT AND KYLE KIMBEL OF THE LOS ANGELES MYCOLOGICAL SOCIETY

2 tablespoons oil
¼ cup minced celery
¼ cup minced onions
2½ tablespoons flour
1 cup boiling chicken stock
2 cups warm milk
½ teaspoon salt
⅛ teaspoon ground nutmeg
⅛ teaspoon white pepper

⅛ teaspoon tarragon
1 teaspoon margarine or butter
2 cups fresh fairy-ring caps
1 tablespoon sherry (optional)
½ cup minced parsley
2 tablespoons toasted almond flakes

Heat the oil in a saucepan. Add the celery and the onions, and cook until the onions are soft and translucent. Add the flour and cook, stirring constantly, for 3 minutes. Be careful not to brown the flour.

Add the boiling chicken stock all at once, rapidly stirring with a wire whisk. Cook until thickened.

Slowly add the warm milk, salt, nutmeg, white pepper, and tarragon.

In a heavy skillet, melt the margarine or butter. Add the mushrooms, and sauté until tender. Add the mushrooms and the sherry to the soup. Sprinkle the top of each bowl with the parsley and the toasted almond flakes.

Additional mushrooms can be sautéed and salted, then floated in the soup.　　　　SERVES 4.

Hedgehog Mushroom *(Dentinum repandum)*

This is the most common and best known of the tooth fungi. Although viewed from above its orange-to-reddish-brown cap makes it look like any number of gilled mushrooms, the tiny white toothlike structures that it has on its underside instead of gills are its mark of distinction. An easy mushroom to overlook, once you notice it you will be pleased. One October, in Stokes Forest, New Jersey, while bending down to pick up another mushroom, I discovered specimens of this attractive orange species and couldn't resist picking them until my basket was overflowing.

Although there are other tooth fungi that have stems, and most are of unknown edibility, there is no look-alike for this orange-capped mushroom, which grows on the ground in wooded areas, coast to coast, from July to November.

This is a good, steady edible; it is popular in Europe and sold canned in France. Some say it is best mixed with other mushrooms.

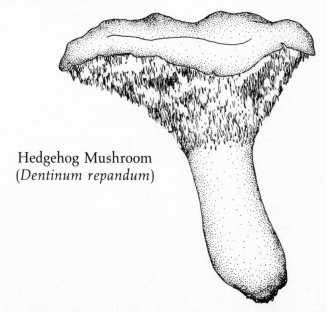

Hedgehog Mushroom
(Dentinum repandum)

Dentinum Orientale (side dish)
FROM THE OREGON MYCOLOGICAL SOCIETY NEWSLETTER

¼ pound butter
¼ medium head
cauliflower, sliced thin
1 zucchini, sliced
6 green onions (scallions), chopped
2 cups sliced *Dentinum repandum*

4 stalks celery, sliced thin
2 carrots, thinly sliced
1 green pepper, sliced
2 tablespoons water (optional)

Combine all the vegetables in a large bowl.

In a skillet, melt the butter. Add the vegetables and mushrooms and sauté 5 minutes. Add mushrooms and continue to cook 1–2 minutes, tossing gently. If dry, add 2 tablespoons water. SERVES 6.

Hen-of-the-Woods *(Grifola frondosa)*

This smoky, gray-capped polypore with a white pore surface resembles a mass of ruffled feathers nesting at the base of a tree. Its small, flat, overlapping caps fan out in clusters that often reach a size of up to several feet. Growing at the bases of oaks and other trees, this fall mushroom is primarily an eastern species in the United States, unknown in California and the Pacific Northwest; it is common in Europe and Japan, where it is cultivated and prized. It is said that this mushroom is so popular in Italy that it is permitted to grow unchecked in chestnut orchards, where the parasitic mycelia destroy the trees.

The hen-of-the-woods has no toxic look-alikes and,

except for the spring and summer mushroom *Polyporus umbellatus*, has no real look-alikes at all.

When cooking the mushroom, only the tender fronds should be used. The base is excellent for soups and stocks only. It is a lovely addition to chicken or veal and is excellent in casseroles. Hen-of-the-woods can be frozen and is excellent pickled. Like most polypores, it doesn't dry well.

Hen-of-the-Woods (*Grifola frondosa*)

Chicken with Hen-of-the-Woods (entrée)
FROM ARLINE AND WALTER DEITCH OF THE NEW YORK MYCOLOGICAL SOCIETY

1 frying chicken, cut up
1½–2 cups sliced hen-of-the-woods
1 pinch MBT powdered chicken broth (optional)
3 tablespoons butter
About ¼ cup chopped shallots

⅓ cup sherry
½ cup chicken stock
2 tablespoons sliced almonds
2 tablespoons sour cream
Salt and pepper to taste

Broil the chicken pieces seasoned with salt, pepper, and a sprinkling of the MBT powder, until the chicken is half-cooked (about 15 minutes). Remove from the oven.

While the chicken is broiling, sauté the shallots in 2 tablespoons butter in a flameproof casserole large enough for chicken. Add the mushroom pieces, and sauté briefly. Add the sherry, chicken stock, broiled chicken pieces, and accumulated juices from the pan; cover and stew until tender (about 15 minutes).

Meanwhile, in a separate pan, sauté the sliced almonds in 1 tablespoon butter until golden brown and set aside. When the chicken is tender, add the sour cream to sauce and stir vigorously with wire whisk until smooth. Sprinkle the sliced almonds over the chicken. SERVES 4.

Baked Hen-of-the-Woods (side dish)
FROM ZACHARY SKLAR

3 scallions, chopped
(green part as well)
¼ teaspoon fresh ginger
3 tablespoons butter
1½ cups sliced young tips
of hen-of-the-woods
4 cherry tomatoes, halved

1 clove garlic, crushed
1 sprig chopped coriander
leaves
¼ cup grated Gruyère
cheese
Salt and pepper to taste

Preheat over to 350°F.

Sauté in butter the scallions, the ginger, and the garlic. Add the mushrooms, and sauté until tender. Add the remaining ingredients and bake for about 30 minutes. SERVES 4.

Honey Mushroom *(Armillariella mellea)*

If I had to choose one fungus as the quintessential wild mushroom, it would be the honey. It is everywhere. In France it is called *Armillaire tête de méduse;* in Germany, *Lallmasch;* in Sweden, *Honungskivling.* To the Italians, *chiodino* on pasta comes close to heaven. To the rest of us, it is a fine edible when properly cooked.

The honey mushroom is tenacious, rapacious, and ubiquitous. To the plant pathologist, it is a virulent parasite working its way by means of rootlike black structures through tree roots, bark, and open tree wounds. But it can also act as a saprophyte, helping to decay dead trees, and work in mycorrhizal concert with certain orchids, ensuring their growth.

Over time, and from cluster to cluster, the honey changes appearance like a chameleon. The color is usually golden, but not always. Erect black hairs form on the cap but are not always clearly apparent without a hand lens. The honey grows clustered on stumps and trees, but sometimes it is scattered on buried wood. The ring varies from white to yellowish. The stem is sometimes long and thin, sometimes stout and tapered. The whitish gills may become partly decurrent and discolor to yellowish or rusty brown. This tremendous variation has led taxonomists to conclude that they are dealing with seven or eight different species, but most amateurs ignore the professionals' fine distinctions and continue to treat the honey as one.

The variations can also lead even experienced mushroom hunters to confuse the honey with a few toxic mushrooms that also grow on wood in the fall and that

Honey Mushroom (*Armilleriella mellea*)

to varying degrees vaguely resemble the honey. Careful examination of the mushroom and the taking of spore prints should eliminate mistakes.

Mistakes can lead to an out-of-body experience, a gastrointestinal catastrophe, or a potentially deadly experience. The most common mistake is confusing the honey with the jack o'lantern. White-spored like the honey, the jack o'lantern also grows in clusters on stumps, logs, and at the bases of trees, but it is distinguished by the yellow-orange gills that descend down its stem. The jack o'lantern is ringless, unlike the honey, and if you care to take it home for further proof, wait until dark and the gills may give off an eerie, green glow.

Another more serious, but far less obvious, look-alike of the honey is the *Galerina autumnalis (marginata* or *venenata),* a small fall complex of species that grows on wood. The *Galerina* contains amatoxins that can be deadly in large enough doses. But the mushrooms in this genus have a brown spore print and the fragile remnant of a ring; they grow scattered or in groups, never clustered as the honey and the jack o'lantern are. Although it is not commonly mistaken for the honey, I do know of one instance where it was—which was bad enough to validate all the warnings.

Verified honey in hand, now what? This is a mushroom that must be cooked thoroughly—some say for up to fifteen minutes. Eaten raw, undercooked, or *al dente,* the mushroom can cause upset stomach. Young buttons are best; older specimens tend to get slightly acrid and glutinous.

Honeys are excellent in soup; they are delicious, of course, sautéed with pasta, and they make a good stir-fry. They can be preserved by sautéeing lightly in peanut oil and soy sauce and then freezing, pickling, or canning.

It might seem that after all these caveats, the honey is hardly worthwhile. On the contrary, it is a plentiful, popular, versatile mushroom, and with a little care you will have a full winter supply of ingredients for stews and ragouts, quiches, duxelles, and omelettes.

Pickled Honeys
FROM DR. ORSON MILLER

1 cup vinegar
½ cup sugar
1 teaspoon mixed pickling
  spices
2 cups *Armillariella*
  mellea buttons

1 dried hot red pepper
  (optional)
Salt to taste

Simmer all ingredients except the mushrooms 2–3 minutes.

Add the mushrooms. Make sure the pickling solution covers them. Simmer 10–20 minutes. Pour into sterilized jars and seal.

King Bolete, or Cep *(Boletus edulis)*

John Cage, composer and devoted mycophile, tells of a time during the Depression when he subsisted for a week on a diet of wild fungi. He knew nothing of mushrooms at the time, but was living near Carmel, California, where the woods and lawns were covered with them. He picked a few specimens and went to the library, where he discovered in a field guide that these spongy-bottom mushrooms are boletes and that they are safe to eat. After the week was up, Cage was still alive, but in a greatly weakened condition. Although this story doesn't say much

Cep (*Boletus edulis*)

for the nutritional value of mushrooms in general, it does say a lot for the safety of eating boletes.

Most genera and species of bolete that grow in this country are edible and taste good. A few red-pored or blue-staining species are toxic no matter how you cook them, a few others will cause discomfort if you eat them raw or undercooked. Several other species are distasteful *(Gyrodon merulioides)* or tasteless; others are bitter (several species of *Tylopilus*, especially *felleus*), but it is easy enough to find these out by tasting them. A larger problem with boletes generally is that insects and other small creatures seem to find them as tasty as we do. There are few things more disappointing than to come upon a dozen healthy-looking large boletes, only to pick them and have them turn to mush in your hand, or to cut them open and find a rush-hour traffic circle of larva tunnels running right through the flesh.

For most mycophagists, there are many equally choice boletes. By common agreement, however, there is one that stands out as king among kings. It is *Boletus edulis*, known also as the cep, *Steinpilz, prawdziwek*, and by a dozen other names. It is the bolete you expect to be buying dried in specialty food stores. But be wary, for like many wines and truffles, a package that says "Ceps" often includes a rather large percentage of others. (Harmless it may be, but legal it isn't.)

Like most other boletes, the cep grows under conifers and deciduous trees from June through October in most parts of the country, and in late fall through winter in California. It is a variable mushroom with a smooth cap ranging from red-brown to tawny to chestnut to dark brown. The flesh is white, and the pores are white when young, turning to tawny with age. The stem can be short or long and is usually stout or bulbous. Just under the cap on the top of the stem are white or pale-colored web-like hairs called reticulations.

There is one major look-alike for *B. edulis*, and although confusion won't result in a serious problem, it can be very frustrating. *Tylopilus felleus*, known appropriately as the bitter bolete, is similar in general appearance to the cep. Its cap color and stalk shape both vary in the same way, and the mushroom has webbing on the upper stem. But the reticulation on *T. felleus* is dark, and the mushroom's pores are pinkish. If you have any doubts, just take a small bite. *T. felleus* has a disagreeable bitterness that cannot be disguised or cooked out.

Many experienced mycophagists insist that the cep is far better dried than fresh. The flavor, they say, is enhanced, and the reconstituted mushroom does not have that soggy texture common to so many fresh boletes. There are many ways to cook boletes, but it seems that everyone has at least one soup recipe. (There is something about this mushroom that just seems to go with soup.) The flavor is so strong that a mere few will go a long way. Arline and Walter Deitch, former presidents of the New York Mycological Society, report that they kept their boletes on a string to dry, using two or three each time they made a new bowl of soup. After the mushrooms were gone, they cooked the string. Although the flavor wasn't quite as intense, they admitted, it definitely added a distinct bolete taste.

Mushroom Barley Soup
FROM SYLVIA STEIN OF THE CONNECTICUT MYCOLOGICAL ASSOCIATION

1 ounce dried cep	6 cups water
1 pound beef flanken	Beef stock or bouillon for
¼ cup barley	flavor
2 onions, cut up	Salt and pepper to taste

Crumble the dried mushrooms. Soak them to remove grit. Strain and reserve the liquid.

In a pot, place the meat, water, and liquid and bring to boil. Remove the scum as it rises to the top. Add the rest of the ingredients, and cook for a couple of hours until the meat is tender. Adjust the seasonings. Cover partly during cooking, and add more water if necessary. Season with salt and pepper.   SERVES 4.

Lobster Mushroom *(Hypomyces lactifluorum)*

A bright orange mushroom that grows among the leaves on roadsides and on the woodland floor, this bulky, fluted mushroom is actually two fungi: a colorful mold or parasite grows on various species of *Lactarius* and *Russula* throughout North America during the summer months. In this case, the parasite turns an unpalatable host into a choice edible.

The lobster mushroom grows from coast to coast; in the Northwest, it is a bigger, denser mushroom, with a chalklike texture when eaten; it tends to be less popular than in the eastern United States.

The texture and taste of this mushroom are meaty. It is best sautéed slowly and makes a lovely dish when served with noodles. In sufficient quantities, it holds its own with strongly flavored meats and sauces.

Lobster Mushroom Appetizer
FROM JOHN CAGE

2 good-size lobster
mushrooms, cut in ½"
slices

2 tablespoons sesame oil
2 teaspoons hot mustard
or tamari

Clean and prepare the mushrooms. Brush them with sesame oil.

Broil or grill them quickly and brush again with tamari or hot mustard. SERVES 4.

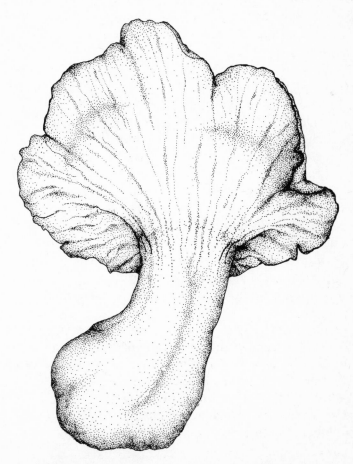

Lobster Mushroom (*Hypomyces lactifluorum*)

Meadow Mushroom
(Agaricus campestris)

This is the wild first cousin of the familiar bland supermarket staple. Suburbanites find it on their lawns, and even big-city dwellers find it in parks, vacant lots, and traffic islands. The next time you buy a package of supermarket mushrooms, examine them carefully. Take a spore print. They are a close relative of the meadow mushroom and will help you become familiar with its characteristics.

Although *Agaricus campestris* is the best-known and most widely gathered member of the genus *Agaricus*, there are many other species that are equally edible and taste even better: *arvensis*, *augustus*, and *silvicola*, for example. A few are toxic, causing stomach upset; *A. californicus* is one of these. A dead ringer for the meadow mushroom, *californicus* grows only in California (largely in urban parks and lawns) and can be distinguished by its pungent odor.

Once you are familiar with this mushroom, it's hard to imagine that it could be confused with a deadly white *Amanita*, but that is always a concern for beginners. Caution is called for. Take spore prints when in doubt, check the gill color, and use your field guide to be absolutely sure.

A mild-mannered mushroom, *Agaricus campestris* is still more assertive than its supermarket cousin, and it can hold its own in a tasty tomato sauce. Young specimens are far more flavorful, and the mushroom is best cooked right away, sautéed or in eggs or other lightly seasoned dishes. To preserve them, sautéeing, or parboiling and then freezing, or drying work fine.

Fungi La Fonda (side dish)
FROM TOM FLYNN OF THE COLORADO MYCOLOGICAL SOCIETY

1 pound *Agaricus campestris*, sliced or whole buttons
4 tablespoons butter
2 tablespoons olive oil
1 clove garlic, mashed

¼ cup parsley, finely chopped
½ cup white vermouth (or any good white wine)
1 tablespoon lemon juice

Combine the butter, olive oil, and garlic over medium heat until the foam subsides and garlic is lightly colored. Add the mushrooms and the parsley. Simmer 3–4 minutes, uncovered.

Add the lemon juice and the vermouth. Cook another 3–4 minutes.

Serve at once with French bread to dip into the juices. SERVES 4.

Meadow Mushroom
(*Agaricus campestris*)

Greek Mushrooms (side dish)
FROM FRAN SHINAGEL OF THE NEW YORK MYCOLOGICAL SOCIETY

1 pound fresh young
Agaricus campestris
caps
2 tablespoons finely
chopped shallots

3–4 tablespoons olive oil
Salt and pepper to taste
¼ cup parsley, finely
chopped

Combine all the ingredients except the parsley in a medium-size noncorrosive saucepan. Cover, bring to a simmer, and cook until tender, about 5 minutes.

Sprinkle with the parsley. Serve room temperature.

SERVES 4.

Morel *(Morchella esculenta* or *deliciosa)*

To many, this spongy-capped creature is the Moby Dick, the Holy Grail, the El Dorado of mushrooms. Even where it is plentiful, mushroom hunters will lie, cheat, and steal for a mouthful—or a ton. Generous to a fault about revealing their sites for other kinds of mushrooms, morel hunters threaten to shoot on sight any person caught poaching on their territory. To others, including many of us in the eastern United States, morels are more like UFOs: we are certain only that *others* have seen them. Back East, we count them; in the West, they weigh them. I have always believed that obsession is a result of unavailability, but judging from the way the large quantities found in Michigan and northern California are still treasured, there must be something magical about the mushroom itself.

Morel season lasts for approximately three weeks in

the spring. These three weeks fall at different times in different regions of the continent. They may begin as early as March in Los Angeles and North Carolina and end as late as June or July in Canada. Morels are found in the Rockies as late as August. Part of the attraction of morels is the mystery that surrounds their location. They are said to grow in old apple orchards, under tulip poplars and near dead elms, on banks and under hedges, under ash, walnut, and butternut, in conifer woods, in swampy places, and in construction sites. So where are they? With all our clues, we find them, if at all, where and when they choose to appear. Tracking morel migration routes can become a serious obsession. One New Jersey amateur bought a topographical map of the state

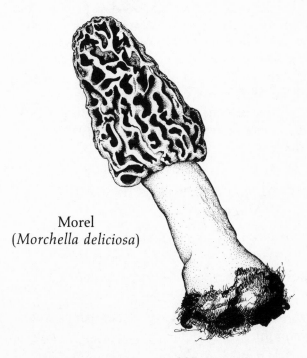

Morel
(*Morchella deliciosa*)

and put pins in the areas where he had found morels. All morel areas, he discovered, were rich in limestone.

Morels vary in size and shape, and their colors range from pale gold to near black. But their most distinctive features are consistent: an egg-shaped-to-conical head of ridges and pits and a hollow cap and stem.

Beginners are always warned to look out for the *Gyromitra*, a fleshy Ascomycete of rather dubious reputation. Once you have seen them both, however, I believe there is no danger of mistaking one for the other. The cap of the *Gyromitra* is more brain-shaped than spongy, and it is not hollow when you cut it open.

Although there is no dispute among mycophagists as to the desirability of eating morels, they do split into two camps on *how* to eat them. Some people prefer morels fresh, while others say that the woodsy flavor is enhanced by drying and then rehydrating them in water, wine, or cream. Some devotees insist that morels are so good that they should be eaten alone, sautéed in butter and shallots, and then served on toast points or stuffed—with chopped morels, of course—and then baked or broiled. Others, less purist, are perfectly satisfied cooking morels in cream sauce and serving them with veal.

Morel Canapés (appetizer)
FROM MARGARET LEWIS OF THE BOSTON MYCOLOGICAL SOCIETY

2 ounces dried morels reconstituted in ¼ cup hot water until soft (save liquid)
½ ounce minced shallots
Splash lemon juice
2 ounces chicken stock

6 tablespoons butter
5 tablespoons flour
2 ounces Madeira or sherry
1 tablespoon parsley, minced finely
Salt and pepper to taste

2 ounces morel	16 slices thin sandwich
2 ounces cream	bread

Drain morels, chop, sauté with shallots in 1 tablespoon butter, about 5 minutes over low flame. Add splash of lemon juice and continue cooking for 10 minutes longer.

Make cream sauce in double boiler: Melt butter, add flour and stir, adding morel juice, chicken stock, and cream. Simmer until thick. Add sautéed morels and shallots and add salt, pepper, wine, and parsley. Cool.

Remove crusts and butter very thin slices of white bread. Cover with morel sauce. Butter top slice and cover sauce. Cut into 8 triangles. Place in moderate oven until browned.

Grete's Morel Ragout (entrée)
FROM GRETE TURCHICK OF THE NEW JERSEY MYCOLOGICAL SOCIETY

1 pound of veal for stewing	2 tablespoons butter
2 cups water	2 tablespoons flour
½ teaspoon salt	1 cup heavy cream
1 pound morels	2 egg yolks
4 baked pastry shells	Salt to taste

Simmer the veal in water with salt for 1 hour, or until tender. Remove from the pan, reserving the broth, and cut into cubes.

Wash the morels and chop them coarsely. Simmer for about 10 minutes in the veal broth. Drain, and reserve the broth.

In a saucepan, melt the butter; add the flour and cook until lightly colored. Add the broth and salt. Whisk vigorously to combine. Add the veal and the morels to the sauce. Heat 5–10 minutes.

Combine the heavy cream and the egg yolks. Add them to the creamed mixture. Fill the pastry shells with the mixture. SERVES 4.

Orange Milky *(Lactarius deliciosus)*

The sight of the orange milky hiding among conifers during late summer and fall never fails to bring delighted "aahs" from diligent foragers. As with so many other mushrooms, the first one is the hardest to spot, and more often than not a little digging among the pine duff will produce more—if you're lucky, more than a dozen.

Like many other species of the genus *Lactarius, L. deliciosus,* when young, has a convex cap marked with dark zones and an inrolled edge. As it ages, the cap opens its edges and inverts, giving it a vaselike shape. Mushrooms of the genus *Lactarius* produce a latex or milk on their gills that can be white, yellow, blue, or, in the case of *deliciosus,* orange fading to yellowish and then turning green and staining the yellow flesh. Its fruity odor is unmistakable, and as long as the milk is present there is no serious contender for a toxic look-alike. There are three other *Lactarii* that are similar in appearance and equally delicious: *volemus, corrugis,* and *hygrophoroides,* all of which have white milk; the first two have an unmistakable fishy odor.

Charles McIlvaine says of this mushroom, "It requires forty minutes stewing or baking; less time if roasted or fried. It can be cooked any way, but like all *Lactarii* must be well-cooked." Others have said that the mushroom is

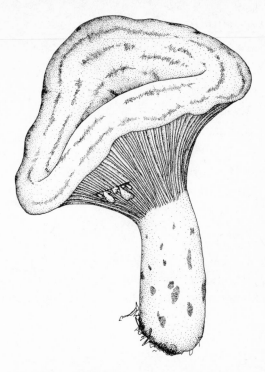

Orange Milky (*Lactarius deliciosus*)

best sautéed—adding cumin and coriander—but is not especially good in other dishes. Some find that the latex has a bitter taste. To remove this, you can boil the mushroom whole in salted water and then drain it before using. One summer weekend, two stranded foragers, having discovered themselves with a dead car battery, a basketful of *L. deliciosus*, and an empty cabin with no culinary condiments, roasted the mushrooms on sticks over the fire. They claim to have invented a new delicacy. I also hear that this mushroom is excellent with venison.

Champignon Alla Plancha (side dish)
FROM R. LEHMAN OF THE COLORADO MYCOLOGICAL SOCIETY

2 pounds *Lactarius deliciosus*, cut up
3 tablespoons butter
1 teaspoon sesame oil
1 clove garlic, chopped

¾ cup chopped parsley
1 cup dry white wine
Salt and pepper to taste
½ cup water chestnuts (optional)

Combine the butter and oil in a skillet and sauté the garlic quickly until it shows slight color. Add the mushrooms and parsley, and sauté on high heat until the mushrooms begin to release water. Add the wine, salt, pepper, and water chestnuts if desired. Cover the skillet and simmer until the mushrooms are tender. Correct the seasoning and serve hot.　　　SERVES 4.

Oyster Mushroom *(Pleurotus ostreatus or sapidus)*

One May Sunday, I collected about twenty pounds of these scallop-shaped white mushrooms from a large oak tree in Central Park. Poking and prodding with a long branch, I attracted an amused crowd that stopped mostly to stare, but some helped and others asked questions. Eventually, a chic middle-aged woman approached and said with the enthusiasm of recognition, "Oh, those look just like the oyster mushrooms I buy at Balducci's"— referring to an expensive specialty food shop in Manhattan's Greenwich Village. "They are," I answered, "but these are fresher—and cheaper. Here, take some." I held out a dozen perfect specimens for her. "Oh, no, I couldn't." She refused, politely backing away. "How do I know they're not poisonous?"

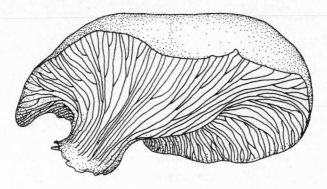

Oyster Mushroom (*Pleurotus ostreatus*)

The oyster, a wood decomposer, is widely cultivated by both professionals and amateurs. It fruits rapidly and grows on many combinations of media—straw, sawdust, logs, paper, and/or cornmeal. One California woman reports that she found it growing out of an old kitchen chair she had stored in her basement.

In the wild, the oyster is one of the easiest mushrooms to recognize. The cluster of copious overhanging shelves is difficult to miss, sometimes covering a whole stump or the trunk of an oak, willow, aspen, or other deciduous tree. Although the cap color ranges from white to brown, its oyster-shell shape is constant. The mushroom is sometimes stalkless and at other times has a short or off-center stem. The gills are white and widely spaced. The spore print is white in *ostreatus* and lilac in *sapidus*. The season is long—from May to December—giving hope to a cold, winter walk in the woods.

Like most edibles, the oyster is best collected when young. It tends to get tough with age, and it attracts large beetle colonies or can develop a yellow slimy substance. The slime can be cut off, and if soaked in salt water, the beetles will float to the surface. McIlvaine says of the oyster, "The camel is gratefully called the ship of the desert; the oyster mushroom is the shellfish of the forest. When the tender parts are dipped in egg, rolled in bread crumbs, and fried as an oyster, they are not excelled by any vegetable, and are worthy of a place in the daintiest menu."

As its name suggests, the oyster is a favorite addition to seafood. Sautéed with a touch of lemon, it goes well with scalloped veal. The tougher base can be used for soup. Margaret Lewis of Boston, the septuagenarian mycophagist whose cooking classes have waiting lists of up to three years, sautés the tender oyster and serves it in a scallop shell. "I swear," she insists, "that no one can tell the difference."

Oysters For Sure—Well, They Were (appetizer)
FROM MARGARET LEWIS OF THE BOSTON MYCOLOGICAL SOCIETY

1 dozen oysters (save juice and shells)
2 dozen small oyster mushroom caps
4 tablespoons butter
1 teaspoon chopped shallots
⅓ onion, finely chopped
⅓ cup Muscadet or dry white wine
½ cup breadcrumbs
Splash of cognac
2 tablespoons fresh parsley, chopped
8 crushed fennel seeds
1½ tablespoons veal or chicken stock

Preheat oven to 350°F.
Simmer the oysters, in water to cover, 1–2 minutes

and transfer them with a slotted spoon to a bowl. In a pan, combine the oyster juice from the raw oysters, 2 tablespoons butter, shallots, onion, Muscadet, fennel seeds, mushroom caps, and stock. Simmer for about 20 minutes over very low heat until the juice has been reduced to a scant amount.

Place one oyster in each shell with one oyster mushroom cap on each side. Divide the shallots evenly and place on each oyster. Splash each shell with flamed cognac. Combine remaining butter, breadcrumbs, and parsley. Sprinkle a little breadcrumb mixture on top of each oyster.

Bake about 10 minutes or until golden.   SERVES 4.

Parasol *(Lepiota procera)*

Until I was introduced to the Western matsutake and *Catathelasma,* the parasol had always been my favorite edible. I am still drawn to its delicate beauty and earthy flavor.

In the eastern United States, the parasol is plentiful during summer and fall but not so common as to be boring. It grows singly and in scattered groups, and sometimes even as fairy rings in grassy areas. It is one of the few mushrooms that seems to prefer sun to shade.

Despite its ring, its free white gills, and its white spore print, the parasol bears little resemblance to the destroying angel. The cap of the *Lepiota* is covered with reddish brown scales and has an umbo, or nipple, in the center. The stalk is long, very slender, and scaly, unlike the smooth, more stately stem of the destroying angel. The parasol ring, which usually detaches and can be moved by hand up and down the stem, reminds me more of a wedding ring or of a rolled-down stocking than of the

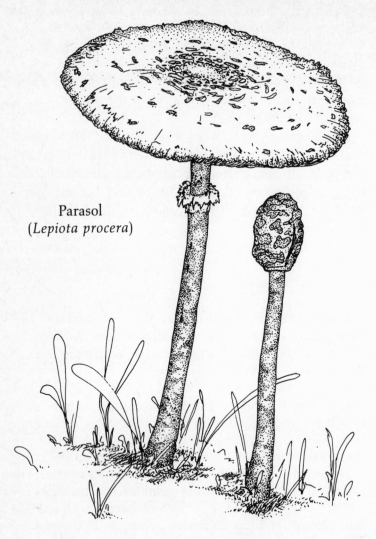

Parasol
(*Lepiota procera*)

torn skirtlike ring of the *Amanita*. And while the stalk of the parasol is slightly bulbous at the base, it is not covered by a volva.

The parasol does, however, have a toxic look-alike, the

Chlorophyllum molybdites, also called the green-spored *Lepiota.* If you look carefully, you can see the telltale difference—the green tint on the gills—and if you take a spore print, you'll see the greenish spores produced by the toxic mushroom.

Parasol caps have been known to come as big as twenty inches in diameter. Broiled or stuffed, they make a full meal for two. They preserve well if frozen or dried, although in our house they never lasted long enough to tell. Whenever my son Michael discovered a jar of parasols, he quickly got over his fear and loathing of wild mushrooms. One evening, while watching television, he devoured our entire winter collection as if it were a bag of potato chips.

I prefer this strongly flavored mushroom simply sliced and sautéed, or grilled whole if the caps are large enough, with a sprinkling of cheese or a meat-and-nut stuffing.

Lepiota Topping (appetizer)
FROM RICHARD KOEPPEL

4 large (or 8 small) fresh parasol caps	1 tin of foie gras
1 artichoke bottom, cut in four pieces	3 tablespoons butter
	Salt and pepper to taste
	Madeira wine

Sauté the fresh parasols in 2 tablespoons of butter with salt and pepper about 5 minutes or until they are done—slightly browned on the gills. Serve on a sautéed artichoke bottom.

Top this with a thin slice of warmed foie gras, and serve with a sauce made from the Madeira and remaining butter.   SERVES 4.

Puffball *(Lycoperdon pyriforme)*

There are many species of the stalkless, round-to-pear-shaped, white-to-buff-colored, and marble-to-boulder-size puffball that are edible and choice. This particular species, *L. pyriforme*, is among the most abundant and easiest to recognize. Pear-shaped, as its species name, *pyriforme*, suggests, it is usually found in sparkling clusters on logs or rotten wood. White and warted when young, the mushroom turns yellow-green as it matures. Like many other puffballs, it grows from May to November throughout North America.

As with all puffballs, only the young are edible. Firm outside, with a white, cheesy consistency inside, the yellowish mush that they turn to in age is undesirable as well as inedible. Puffballs are delicious cooked in many ways, but one of the most popular is to slice them thinly, dip them in egg and breadcrumbs, and sauté them in butter. They can be sautéed, dried, pickled, or frozen to preserve.

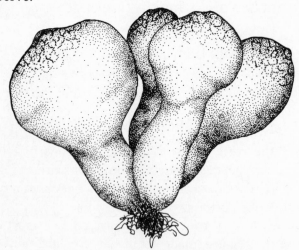

Puffball (*Lycoperdon pyriforme*)

Puffball Casserole (side dish)
From the New Jersey Mycological Society
newsletter

3 cups sliced puffballs
1 egg
6–7 tablespoons butter
½–¾ cup breadcrumbs

1 cup milk
½–¾ cup Parmesan
   cheese, grated
Salt and pepper to taste

Preheat oven to 350°F.
Layer the puffball slices and breadcrumbs in the bottom of a casserole dish, dotting each layer with butter.
Beat together the egg and milk and add enough to cover, with salt and pepper, to the mushrooms.
Sprinkle the top with the grated cheese. Bake 20 minutes or until a knife placed in the custard comes out clean.   serves 4.

Macrobiotic Puffball Lasagna (entrée)
From John Cage

3 cups large puffball cut
   into ½–¾" slices (or
   enough to use as
   "pasta")
2 cups coarsely chopped
   mixture of any
   varieties of edible
   mushrooms

¼ cup sesame oil
2 tablespoons tamari
2 cups tofu and miso
   mixture (should be
   consistency of cheese)

Preheat oven to 350°F.

Place layer of puffball slices in lasagna pan. Sautée other mushrooms in sesame oil. Add tamari to mushrooms. Alternate puffball layer, with mushrooms and then tofu-miso mixture.

Cook 45 minutes to 1 hour, or until the lasagna is well amalgamated.   SERVES 4.

Shaggy Mane *(Coprinus comatus)*

This mushroom is ethereal-looking, exquisitely edible, easy to recognize, and anatomically intriguing. Scores of these shaggy white mushrooms appear out of nowhere, like ants at a June picnic, all over lawns, golf courses, roadsides, and other grassy areas after heavy rains. Perfect city mushrooms, they also grow in vacant lots, housing project lawns, parks, and dumps. Despite their delicate appearance, shaggy manes and other members of the genus *Coprinus* are quite tenacious, thriving in hard-packed soil; they are even known to push up through hundreds of pounds of stone pavement or clay tennis court.

Unlike other gilled mushrooms, the *Coprinus* does not release its spores by means of gravity. Under its cone-cap, the gills are pressed together very tightly in a vertical position, leaving very little space for falling spores. The means of spore dispersal for the *Coprinus* is called autodigestion, or deliquescence; the gills literally dissolve into an inky black fluid. As the gills dissolve, the spores contained in the inky fluid drop to the ground. For this reason, many species of *Coprinus* are called inky caps. There are no toxic look-alikes for the shaggy mane.

The whole process of deliquescence can take place in a few hours; it is best to catch shaggy manes and other edible inky caps before they begin to turn black. Some suggest taking a frying pan into the field and cooking

Shaggy mane
deliquescing

Shaggy mane (*Coprinus comatus*)

them there. Others have discovered that such drastic action isn't really necessary. Placed in the refrigerator in a covered jar of cold water, shaggy manes will stay fresh for a week.

These delicately flavored mushrooms can be cooked in a variety of ways. In addition to being sautéed in ghee, or clarified butter, they are delicious in a cream sauce with scrambled eggs, veal, or chicken. I have known people who use them as a substitute for asparagus, to which they are comparable in texture if not in taste or smell. Shaggy manes can be parboiled or sautéed and frozen; they don't dry well.

Baked Shaggy Manes (side dish)
FROM LARRY STICKNEY OF THE SAN FRANCISCO MYCOLOGICAL ASSOCIATION

1 dozen small *Coprinus comatus* caps
4 tablespoons heavy cream

2 tablespoons butter
1–2 tablespoons cognac or armagnac
Salt and pepper to taste

Preheat oven to 350°F.

Trim the mushrooms and wash them carefully. Drain in a colander.

Spread them out in one layer in a casserole. Dust them lightly with salt and pepper, and dot with butter. Cover, and bake for 25 minutes.

Heat the cream and add it to the mushrooms. Add cognac or armagnac.

Serve on toast or rice.   SERVES 4.

Shiitake
(*Lentinus edodes*)

Shiitake *(Lentinus edodes)*

It is ironic, although not very surprising, that the mushroom most responsible for the American consumer's recent "discovery" of the wild mushrooms is not even a native of the United States. The shiitake, whose name means "oak-loving fungus" in Japanese, grows prolifically on oak and many other deciduous trees in China, Japan, and Korea. It has spread to our gourmet shops, vegetable stores, and supermarkets, where this tortoise-shell-capped mushroom, when fresh, is sold for $15 to $20 a pound.

In 1972, a domestic ban on the importation of "living cultures" from foreign countries was lifted, and the U.S. Department of Agriculture began large-scale experiments inoculating logs of oak, willow, maple, and other deciduous trees with shiitake spawn or mycelia. The mushroom fruited beautifully though slowly, as is its nature.

Now commercial enterprises in California, Virginia, Washington, Maryland, Maine, and other states are producing the mushroom and seeking ways to grow it more rapidly. The habitat of our northeastern woods is similar enough to that of Japan that some predict that shiitake spores will take off and become naturalized, growing all by themselves in our native oak woods. So far, it hasn't happened, and while North American mushroom hunters look forward to finding wild shiitake in our woods, we shall for the time being have to settle for finding them in between the coffee bins and the cheese displays.

Like most mushroom hunters, I balk at the idea of buying any mushroom in a store, but I have to admit that I am pleased when friends present me with bags of this fungus. The aroma of the shiitake escapes the package and pervades the room. The taste is as rich as the odor, and only a few are needed to flavor any meal. Shiitake are excellent grilled, broiled, sautéed, or used in spaghetti sauces and stews.

Stuffed Shiitake (vegetable or side dish)
FROM DIANA FRIEDMAN, BERKELEY, CALIFORNIA

12 shiitake cups
⅔ cup finely chopped celery
½ cup butter
⅔ cup finely chopped walnuts
⅔ cup seasoned breadcrumbs

¼ teaspoon nutmeg
⅛ teaspoon allspice
Salt and pepper to taste
2 tablespoons grated Parmesan cheese
2 tablespoons chopped parsley
Lettuce leaves

Preheat oven to 400°F.

Remove and chop the mushroom stems. Sauté the stems, celery, and walnuts in all but a tablespoon of the butter until the celery is tender but not brown. Stir occasionally.

Combine the breadcrumbs, nutmeg, allspice, salt, and pepper. Add to the skillet mixture, stirring very well. Stir in the Parmesan cheese and set aside.

Melt the remaining butter. Dip the mushroom caps in butter and place on a baking sheet. Fill the caps with the seasoned nut-crumb mixture. Bake for 10 minutes. Sprinkle with chopped parsley and serve hot on lettuce leaves. SERVES 4.

CHAPTER 15

Poisonous Mushrooms

THROUGHOUT THIS BOOK, I've portrayed wild mushroom eating as highly pleasurable and safe; yet every chapter contains some reference to poisonous species. The contradiction is more apparent than real. Mycophagy *is* safe, because the dangers are easily avoided by following rule number one of any survivor's handbook: *Don't eat any mushroom you don't absolutely know to be harmless.*

Of the many mushrooms that can cause gastrointestinal upset, most wouldn't even tempt you. What little danger there is comes primarily from the poisonous species that resemble the edibles. For the careful observer, there are always clear distinctions, whether in spore color, habitat, season, or morphological characteristics.

The next section describes six of the most common toxic mushrooms and all of the deadly species found in North America. It lists their edible look-alikes and tells you how to distinguish them. You should always, of course, also check your field guide if you are even the least bit suspicious. No recipes are provided.

Death Cap and Destroying Angel
(Amanitae phalloides, virosa, bisporigera, verna, and ocreata)

Ninety percent of all fatal mushroom poisonings are caused by these *Amanitae*, all of which contain the tell-tale characteristics of the genus: a large basal sac or cup (which can, however, disintegrate underground); a skirt-like ring on the upper stalk (which can be washed off in the rain); free white gills; and a white spore print. Unlike the more notorious but far less dangerous *A. muscaria*, the cap of which is covered with small white patches, the caps of these lethal *Amanitae* are generally smooth, with a patch or two remaining from the universal veil.

The death cap, *A. phalloides*, is a fall mushroom, growing mostly, though not exclusively, under oaks and conifers. Originally a European species, this deadly mushroom seems to have entered the country on imported conifer seedlings in the 1930s. The cap of *A. phalloides* varies from very pale to yellowish green to greenish brown.

The other four deadly *Amanitae*—*verna, virosa, bisporigera*, and *ocreata*—are whiter, a bit taller, and more slender than the death cap. They are difficult to tell apart from one another and justly deserve their collective name: the destroying angel. These mushrooms appear from late June through September in different parts of the United States. *Verna*, for example, appears in the Pacific Northwest and rarely in the East; *virosa*, throughout North America; *bisporigera*, largely in the East; and *ocreata* in the Southwest.

Of the more than fifty species of *Amanita* in North America, only these five are known to be deadly. Others, like *muscaria* and *pantherina*, have caused toxic reactions ranging from severe nausea and vomiting to ex-

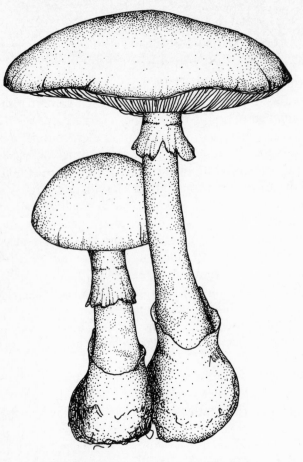

Death Cap (*Amanita phalloides*)

treme disorientation, but they are not known to have caused fatalities. Many other *Amanitae* have never been tested for their toxicity, and several are edible and choice. It is still wise, however, for inexperienced mushroom hunters to limit their collecting of these undetermined *Amanitae* to intellectual satisfaction.

Galerina (Galerina marginata/autumnalis)

Deadly *Galerinae (Galerinae autumnalis, marginata,* and *venenata)*

The principal reason that mushroom hunters are warned to avoid all little brown mushrooms is the toxic wallop packed by these small, brown, innocuous-appearing species. The *Galerinae* all have brown spore prints and a faint ring. *G. autumnalis* and *marginata* grow in spring and fall throughout North America and are usually found in large groups on decaying logs. *G. venenata* is a fall-winter mushroom appearing on lawns in the Northwest. They all contain the same deadly toxins as the *Amanitae,* in the same intensity, but because they are so much smaller it takes more of them to do the same work.

False Morel *(Gyromitra esculenta)*

I find it difficult to understand how this mushroom persists in hanging on to its name. Beyond the fact that they are both spring mushrooms and both fleshy Asco-mycetes, the morel and the *Gyromitra* look very little alike. The morel has a honeycombed cap with pits and ridges, while the cap of *G. esculenta* is wrinkled and brainlike. The morel is hollow inside; the interior of the false morel is chambered.

It is the long-standing mysterious behavior of the *Gyromitra* toxin that can be justly held responsible for so much of the myth and mystique surrounding poisonous mushrooms. For years, this mushroom was known to be fatally toxic to some—even cooks who never tasted it—while others ate it in large quantities with no ill effects. Now that the mystery has been solved, it remains a favorite edible on the West Coast and in Europe and is probably one of the few mushrooms that could fairly be included in both the edible and the poisonous sections of a field guide.

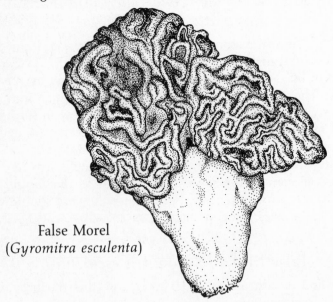

False Morel
(*Gyromitra esculenta*)

Jack O'Lantern (*Omphalotus olearius*)

Jack O'Lantern *(Omphalotus olearius)*

This vase-shaped, stalked, gilled, white-spored, orange mushroom, which can cause a gastric upset that lasts from two hours to two days, is probably responsible for most of the cases of mushroom poisoning in the eastern United States because it is often confused with two of our most common and popular edibles, the chanterelle and the honey mushroom (which are never confused with each other).

Limited to the West and East Coasts, the jack o'lantern is a fall mushroom in the East and a winter mushroom in the West. It is actually two separate species belonging to a complex of similar varieties. Like the honey, and unlike the chanterelle, the jack o'lantern grows on wood, often in very large clusters that sometimes weigh twenty pounds or more. Unlike the honey, and like the chanterelle, the jack o'lantern has no ring. But what really sets this mushroom apart is its bioluminescent character. If you gather it fresh and take a cluster into a dark room, the gills will give off an eerie green glow.

The Sweater *(Clitocybe dealbata)*

This little white mushroom sometimes grows in fairy rings, but the fairies' feet must first have trampled somewhere they shouldn't have. It contains the toxin muscarine, named for *Amanita muscaria*, which stimulates the parasympathetic nerve endings of the autonomic nervous system, and causes profuse glandular secretions that can result in sweating, salivation, and tears, as well as muscle spasms, a slowed heartbeat, and pinpoint pupils. It is the only toxin that responds positively to atropine, the general antidote to mushroom poisoning that in most cases has no effect at all or even exacerbates the condition. Muscarine poisoning also responds to calm, quiet, and the knowledge that it will wear off by itself in about six hours.

The Sweater
(Clitocybe dealbata)

Like all members of the genus *Clitocybe*, this species is marked by decurrent gills, descending partly down the stalk. Like the fairy-ring mushroom, it grows in grassy areas and sometimes in fairy rings. If you are picking *Marasmius*, take a good look at it and carefully read descriptions of both it and the sweater before you serve it on steak.

The Green-Spored
Lepiota (Chlorophyllum molybdites)

This is another strange and fascinating mushroom. It is clearly poisonous, causing several hours of vomiting and diarrhea, yet many people have reported eating it with no ill effects. McIlvaine writes of a woman from Indiana who corresponded with him in 1898 about six families she knew who ate "heartily" of the mushroom. Two members of each family were sick, while the others were fine. The woman herself reported, "I enjoy them immensely. . . . I doubt if we have a finer flavored fungus. The meat is simply delicious." McIlvaine concluded that this green-spored *Lepiota* "contains a poison which violently attacks some persons, yet is harmless upon others." The unpredictable behavior of this mushroom persists and is now attributed as much to geographical distribution as to personal reaction. But despite the good luck of some who eat this mushroom, it is hardly worth the risk. The mushroom is poisonous and should be avoided.

But why do people eat it in the first place? The green-spored *Lepiota* isn't one of those small, innocuous mushrooms that we step on or kick over. It is a large and beautiful white mushroom with a scaly cap and cottony fringes around the edges. In fact, it very closely resembles the parasol and in most cases is probably eaten in error. It is common in some parts of the country, but I have never seen it in the Northeast. I must say, however, that for the first two years I collected and ate parasols, I worried about the confusion and carefully took spore prints of every specimen in my collections. None of them ever came out green.

The Green-Spored *Lepiota*
(*Chlorophyllum molybdites*)

SELECTED BIBLIOGRAPHY

Ainsworth, G. C. *Introduction to the History of Mycology.* Cambridge University Press, 1976.

Alexopoulos, C. J., and C. W. Mims. *Introductory Mycology.* New York: John Wiley & Sons, 1979.

Allegro, John M. *The Sacred Mushroom and the Cross.* New York: Bantam Books, 1971.

Burrell, Robert. *Allergy to Mushrooms: Fact or Fancy?* North American Mycological Association: McIlvainea, 1978.

Carroll, Lewis. *Alice's Adventures in Wonderland.* New York: Mayflower Books, 1980.

Castañeda, Carlos. *The Teachings of Don Juan: A Yaqui Way of Knowledge.* New York: Pocket Books, 1968.

Findlay, W.P.K. *Fungi: Folklore, Fiction and Fact.* England: Richmond Publishing Co., Ltd., 1982.

Findlay, W.P.K. *Wayside and Woodland Fungi.* London: Frederick Warne & Co., Ltd., 1967.

Gwynne-Vaughan, H.C.I. *The Structure and Development of the Fungi.* Cambridge University Press, 1965.

Krieger, Louis C. C. *The Mushroom Handbook.* New York: Dover Publications, 1967.

Largent, David. *How to Identify Mushrooms to Genus III (Microscopic Features).* Eureka, Calif.: Mad River Press.

Lincoff, Gary, and D. H. Mitchell. *Toxic and Hallucinogenic Mushroom Poisoning.* New York: Van Nostrand Reinhold, 1977.

Menser, Gary P. *Hallucinogenic and Poisonous Mushroom Field Guide.* Berkeley, Calif.: And/Or Press, 1977.

Ott, Johnathan, and Jeremy Bigwood (eds.). *Teonanacatl: Hal-*

lucinogenic Mushrooms of North America. Seattle: Madrona Publishers, 1978.

Parker, Loni, and David Jenkins. *Mushrooms, A Separate Kingdom*. Alabama: Oxmoor House, 1979.

Peterson, Ronald. *Name Changes: Woe is Me*. American Mycological Association: McIlvainea, 1980.

Ramsbottom, John. *Mushrooms & Toadstools*. London: Readers Union-Collins, 1960.

Rinaldi, Augusto, and Vassili Tyndalo. *The Complete Book of Mushrooms*. New York: Crown Publishers, 1974.

Rolfe, R. T., and F. W. Rolfe. *The Romance of the Fungus World*. New York: Dover Publications, 1974.

Schultes, R. E. *Hallucinogenic Plants*. New York: Golden Press, 1976.

Schultes, R. E., and A. Hofmann. *Plants of the Gods*. New York: McGraw-Hill, 1979.

Smith, Alexander H. *A Field Guide to Western Mushrooms*. University of Michigan Press, 1975.

Smith, Alexander H., Helen V. Smith, and Nancy Weber. *How to Know the Gilled Mushrooms*. Wm. C. Brown, 1979.

Smith, Helen V., and Alexander H. Smith. *How to Know the Non-Gilled Fleshy Fungi*. Wm. C. Brown, 1973.

Stamets, Paul. *Psilocybe Mushrooms and their Allies*. Seattle: Homestead Books, 1978.

Stuntz, Daniel E. *How to Identify Mushrooms to Genus IV (Keys to Families and Genera)*. Eureka, Calif.: Mad River Press.

Tanghe, Leo J. *Spread of Amanita Phalloides in North America*. North American Mycological Association: McIlvainea, 1983.

Wasson, R. Gordon. *Soma, the Divine Mushroom of Immortality*. San Diego: Harcourt Brace Jovanovich.

Wasson, R. Gordon, and Valentina Wasson. *Russia, Mushrooms and History*. New York: Pantheon Books, 1957.

Watling, Roy. *Identification of the Larger Fungi*. England: Hulton Educational Publications, 1973.

Suggested Field Guides

Arora, David. *Mushrooms Demystified*. Berkeley, Calif.: Ten Speed Press, 1979.

Lincoff, Gary. *The Audubon Society Field Guide to North American Mushrooms*. New York: Alfred A. Knopf, 1981.

McIlvaine, Charles, and Robert Macadam. *One Thousand American Fungi*. New York: Dover Publications, 1973.

McKnight, Kent and Vera. *Peterson's Field Guide to Mushrooms*. Boston: Houghton-Mifflin, 1986.

Miller, Orson A., Jr. *Mushrooms of North America*. New York: E.P. Dutton, 1978.

Smith, Alexander. *The Mushroom Hunter's Field Guide*. University of Michigan Press, 1974.